Advance Praise

The Oil Depletion I

At last — a reality check. Are we ready for the coming decline in oil production? No. Can we prepare for it? Yes. That is what *The Oil Depletion Protocol* is all about. This is another cutting-edge work from Richard Heinberg. My congratulations.

— LESTER R. BROWN, President, Earth Policy Institute

Richard Heinberg's earlier book *The Party's Over* set the scene, explaining how the growth of oil supply, which changed the world over the past Century, is giving way to decline from natural depletion. Now, he turns to a sound but simple solution, namely for the countries of the world to agree to cut imports to match what Nature has to offer. It is a well-written readily comprehensible account of a very sensible proposal that ought to be at the head of every government's agenda and may well soon be so as people wake up to the situation and give their governments the mandate for action.

— COLIN J. CAMPBELL, Chairman,
Association for the Study of Peak Oil

More than anyone, Richard Heinberg has awakened us to the terrifying implications of global Peak Oil and the resulting world economic meltdown. Now, in his latest book, he offers a practical, humane strategy for averting this catastrophe. This book should be read by everyone who believes in the potential for human cooperation and ingenuity to overcome the darkest perils we face.

— MICHAEL KLARE, Professor of Peace & World Security Studies, Hampshire College, and author of *Blood and Oil: The Dangers and Consequences of America's Growing Dependency on Imported Petr*

The Oil Depletion Protocol is set to become a vital tool in the world's attempts to adapt to global oil decline — truly a plan for a sensible energy future. It is clear and conceptually simple in such a way that it can be adopted at every level from international to individual. Get your city, state, and country to adopt the Protocol now!

— JULIAN DARLEY, Post Carbon Institute, and author of *High Noon for Natural Gas*

Stop what you are doing and read this book. It's the clearest explanation of arguably the most devastating crisis of our lifetimes, and it also illuminates the most practical pathway to avert catastrophe. Whatever your field, from business to environment to agriculture, this book will inform all your thinking about the future from here on, and your personal and political engagements in the next crucial decades, as nothing else in print.

— JERRY MANDER, founder, International Forum on Globalization; author, *In the Absence of the Sacred* and *Alternatives to Economic Globalization: a Better World Is Possible*

A strategy for a phased and cooperative post-petroleum world is logical, prudent, and in our self-interest. The alternative is to stumble over the edge into economic hardship and international conflict. In contrast, *The Oil Depletion Protocol* describes a graceful path to a world of sustainable prosperity that begins in a dialogue about rational responses to the inevitable decline of petroleum.

—DAVID ORR, Paul Sears Professor of Environmental Studies at Oberlin College and author of *Design on the Edge*

In this inspirational book, Richard Heinberg has carefully examined the imminent peaking of world oil supplies and the potentially awful consequences for humanity. His very positive conclusion is that if we are to avoid massive disruption and strife, then *The Oil Depletion Protocol* represents a straightforward route to minimizing human misery and one that is easy and practical to apply.

— CHRIS SKREBOWSKI, Editor of *Petroleum Review,* and ODAC Board Member

With this book, Richard Heinberg thoughtfully analyzes the critical economic problems that will soon arise when we reach Hubbert's peak in world oil depletion. I highly recommend an equally thoughtful reading of this book.

— HERMAN E. DALY, Professor, School of Public Policy, University of Maryland

Richard Heinberg is the world's pre-eminent author on the looming crisis that global petroleum depletion represents. *The Oil Depletion Protocol* is required reading for political leaders, policy planners and anyone who is hoping for a smooth landing in a world soon to be short on liquid fuels and even shorter on options.

— ANDREW MCNAMARA, MP, Parliament of Queensland, Australia

Peace and prosperity for your children and grandchildren may be ensured or squandered depending upon whether world leaders commit to work together to overcome the challenges of global peak oil. The United States is the world's largest consumer of oil so Americans have the most to lose from global peak oil — imminent, inevitable and sustained declines in the world supply of conventional oil. Since the U.S. economy is the engine of the world economy, Richard Heinberg's third book about global peak oil, *The Oil Depletion Protocol* should be #1 on the reading list of America's leaders as well as the leaders in every oil-consuming and oil-producing nation. *The Oil Depletion Protocol* provides leaders and citizens a model for discussion and implementation of cooperative steps to reverse the unsustainable trend of increased depletion of the world's rapidly shrinking oil reserves.

— ROSCOE G. BARTLETT, Member of Congress

The proposal to cut oil imports to match depletion rates seems to be simple common sense. I'm happy to support the Protocol outlined in this book.

— THE RIGHT HONOURABLE MICHAEL MEACHER, Member of Parliament, UK

Richard Heinberg leads us with logic into a sobering analysis of where we are and where we must go. The very idea of accepting oil depletion protocols and treaties to guard against irresponsible levels of emissions may not be popular or easily endorsable. Yet, in the annals of history it is clear that epochal crises must be faced. The question is whether they are met with intelligence, resolve, and sacrifice or whether decision makers procrastinate to everyone's eventual peril and suffering. Richard Heinberg's book is a worthy effort to call us to responsible, rational action as an alternative to "letting it happen" and depending on the invisible hand of chaos. *The Oil Depletion Protocol* is very timely — and very cogent.

— THE RIGHT HONOURABLE EDWARD SCHREYER, former Premier of Manitoba, Governor General of Canada, and High Commissioner to Australia and the South Western Pacific

RICHARD HEINBERG

THE OIL DEPLETION PROTOCOL

A PLAN TO AVERT OIL WARS, TERRORISM AND ECONOMIC COLLAPSE

NEW SOCIETY PUBLISHERS

CATALOGING IN PUBLICATION DATA
A catalog record for this publication is available
from the National Library of Canada.

Cover: Composite design and illustration by Diane McIntosh.
Photo: Getty Images/Photodisc Red. Photographer: Christopher Wilhelm.

Printed in Canada.
Second printing September 2006.

Paperback ISBN-13: 978-0-86571-563-9
Paperback ISBN-10: 0-86571-563-7

Inquiries regarding requests to reprint all or part of
The Oil Depletion Protocol should be addressed to
New Society Publishers at the address below.

To order directly from the publishers, please call toll-free
(North America) 1-800-567-6772, or order online at
www.newsociety.com

Any other inquiries can be directed by mail to:
New Society Publishers
P.O. Box 189, Gabriola Island, BC V0R 1X0, Canada
1-800-567-6772

New Society Publishers' mission is to publish books that contribute in
fundamental ways to building an ecologically sustainable and just society,
and to do so with the least possible impact on the environment, in a manner that models this vision. We are committed to doing this not just
through education, but through action. We are acting on our commitment
to the world's remaining ancient forests by phasing out our paper supply
from ancient forests worldwide. This book is one step toward ending
global deforestation and climate change. It is printed on acid-free paper
that is 100% old growth forest-free (100% post-consumer recycled), processed chlorine free, and printed with vegetable-based, low-VOC inks. For
further information, or to browse our full list of books and purchase se-
curely, visit our website at: www.newsociety.com

NEW SOCIETY PUBLISHER   www.newsociety.com

CONTENTS

AUTHOR'S PREFACE

URING THE PAST FIVE YEARS I have become immersed in the subject of Peak Oil, writing two books on the topic and traveling widely to speak to audiences ranging from insurance executives to peace activists, warning of the perils of a lifestyle of oil addiction and of the coming impacts of petroleum depletion. During this time I have come to believe that this is a problem unique in human history, with enormous implications for all components of modern industrial societies. Over the past century we came to rely on a cheap, abundant, and convenient source of energy to fuel economic growth through expanded transportation, industrial agriculture, and ever-diversifying plastics and chemicals industries. Now, as the availability of petroleum enters its inevitable decline, we must find ways to adjust—not only by identifying alternative fuels, but by curtailing many of the activities enabled by this remarkable substance. Doing so will require the coordinated efforts of industry, governments at all levels, and the general populace throughout the world. This will be a daunting challenge, to put it mildly.

Modern societies have faced other challenges in the relatively recent past, including two World Wars and a Great Depression, as well as more localized wars, famines, and natural disasters. Human beings are remarkably adaptable. However in the present instance, the needed adaptation could be profoundly hindered by two likely impacts of Peak Oil—one

economic and the other geopolitical. A protracted and growing global scarcity of the world's most important strategic resource is likely to lead to a meltdown of entire economies,
making needed investments in alternative energy technologies and new post-petroleum infrastructure difficult. At the
same time, competition between major world powers over
remaining oil supplies is likely to increase dramatically and
could escalate into open conflict on a scale never before seen.
This turn of events would have horrific consequences for human beings and the natural world; it would also overwhelm
the ability of any society to accomplish the energy transition
in a coordinated and peaceful manner.

Clearly, humanity needs a way to keep these economic and
political perils at bay while addressing the complex practical
problem of reorganizing its industrial, agricultural, and
transportation infrastructure to function without oil.

In 2002 I became aware that Dr. Colin J. Campbell, the
British petroleum geologist who founded the Association
for the Study of Peak Oil, had authored a Protocol to address
this very situation. I read this Protocol document several
times and came away thinking that here was a good idea with
little chance of being implemented—just another of the
many idealistic proposals that are churned out on a yearly basis by academics, concerned citizens, and small environmental organizations.

Then in May 2005 my wife Janet and I spent two days vis-
iting Colin and Bobbins Campbell in the village of Ballyde-
hob, Ireland, and in one long, illuminating conversation
Colin explained to me how the Protocol would work.

At once I realized that the Oil Depletion Protocol is in fact
practicable, that it would confer immense benefits to signatory nations, and that for the world as a whole it could make

the difference between adaptation and survival on one hand, or chaos and disintegration on the other.

It also became instantly clear that if I—who was devoting myself full-time to talking and writing about Peak Oil—was having trouble understanding the Protocol's implications, then surely much effort would be needed to convey its meaning to the busy policy makers who would have to ratify it, and to the hundreds of millions of citizens who would need to support its ratification in order to embolden their elected representatives.

The Protocol itself is so simple that its essence can be stated in a single sentence: signatory nations would agree to reduce their oil consumption gradually and uniformly according to a simple formula that works out to being a little less than three percent per year. That's almost all there is to it. Why should anyone need further explanation?

If my own experience with the Protocol is any reliable indication, there is in fact substantial need. While the Protocol itself may be straightforward, its historic importance, the means of its implementation, and the implications that flow from it require careful unpacking.

Hence this book.

Throughout the chapters that follow I use the plural pronoun "we" rather than "I" wherever self-reference is necessary simply as a way of acknowledging that, while I am responsible for composing most of the text herein, the book itself represents the work of many. First among these silent co-authors is of course Colin Campbell, who contributed several key draft paragraphs on technical points and was an essential consultant throughout. In addition, I would mention Jennifer Bresee, my research assistant, who not only

found important references but also drafted several paragraphs in Chapters 1, 2, and 4; Julian Darley, Celine Rich-
Darley, and Dave Room of the Post Carbon Institute, the
parent organization of the Oil Depletion Protocol Project;
Pat Murphy, Faith Morgan, and Megan Quinn of the organization Community Solution; members of the Association
for the Study of Peak Oil; and many others who have engaged in discussions over the past year, offering questions
and suggestions about the Protocol.

I would also like to take this opportunity to thank my wife
Janet Barocco, my general assistant Susan Williamson, and
my colleagues and students at New College of California, all
of whom make it possible for me to do this work. Apprecia-
tion is due as well to my publishers, Chris and Judith Plant,
and to Betsy Nuse for her meticulous editing of the
manuscript.

This book is written for both policy makers and the general
public. For the general reader, I have sought to make the
book easy and enjoyable to read, and to provide abundant
references.

For policy makers, I have tried to keep the discussion as
matter-of-fact and as free from political views as possible.
The Oil Depletion Protocol is not a leftist or rightist proposal. It does not try to settle scores. It does not seek to give
more power to those who already have it, or to increase relatively the power of those who have little. What it does—and
all it does—is to offer a plan whereby humankind can survive
the transition away from its dependence on petroleum. All
nations, and all social groups within them, will be better off if
the world adopts such a plan than if it does not.

1

The Challenge of Peak Oil

T HE WORLD IS ENTERING a period of change unlike any
in history. This will be an inherently perilous time, because it will involve a forced and rapid transformation in the
energy system on which our societies and our very lives depend. The transformation will involve the invention of new
technologies and the exploitation of new resources—as was
the case with earlier great economic watersheds. But this time
change will be propelled not merely by new opportunities.
Instead, it will be thrust upon us as a result of the depletion
of the energy resources that enabled the creation of industrial
economies throughout the past two centuries: coal, oil, and
natural gas—though first and foremost, oil.

Oil was the main driver of growth during most of the 20th
Century, and it is the world's primary transportation fuel. We
have become overwhelmingly dependent on this energy-
dense and versatile substance because it is so cheap and convenient as compared with all previous energy sources.

Try the following thought experiment. Perhaps you have had the experience, while driving, of running out of gasoline and having to push your automobile for a few yards. In your mind, extrapolate that experience: imagine pushing your car *twenty miles* (32 kilometers). (It may help to think of two familiar geographical points twenty miles apart). According to the rules of this exercise you may imagine yourself using pulleys or levers to help you move your car up hills, but you may not use engines or fuels of any kind. This is a lot of work—in fact, it represents the energy equivalent of well over a month's hard human labor. Yet this is the service we obtain from a single gallon (3.8 liters) of gasoline, for which we are accustomed to paying only a few dollars at most.

Less than two centuries ago, most of the work done in even the wealthiest nations was accomplished by muscle power, human or animal. But muscles are puny compared to fuel-fed engines. We learned this with engines fed first with wood, then coal. But oil is a fuel superior to either of these. So magical are the benefits of oil that it was inevitable that we would find more and more uses for it. And so we have built an entire way of life around it.

Natural gas and coal, our other principal hydrocarbon fuels, are likewise important non-renewable and depleting energy resources, and they generate similar problems (pollution of various kinds, including climate-changing CO_2). However, in this book we will devote our attention primarily to oil. Our reasons for doing so are: first, that oil's role as transportation fuel has enabled it to play a central role in economic growth, and second, that on a global scale oil's scarcity is likely to affect most societies before scarcities of coal or gas appear.[1] And so oil scarcity, unless we act wisely, could threaten everything we hold dear. This book is therefore about oil depletion—its probable impacts, and especially *what the nations of the world can do to lessen those impacts*.

It is important to understand at the outset that the world is not about to *run out* of oil. There are still many hundreds of billions of barrels[2] of petroleum that can be extracted from the Earth's crust. However, the rate at which oil can be extracted is subject to geological limits, and at some point those limits will begin to constrain our ability to produce oil at the ever-expanding rates that growing economies demand. In other words, the rate of oil production will peak and begin an inevitable decline, for reasons having little to do with economics or technology. There is some disagreement about when those limits will be reached, as we will explore below. Nevertheless, it is quite likely that the time interval before the global peak occurs will be briefer than the period required for societies to adapt themselves painlessly to a different energy regime.

If we are not already doing so, we soon will be entering the transition from a century-and-a-half during which the available supply of oil[3] grew each year, to a future characterized by declining annual supplies. This transition is commonly referred to as Peak Oil.

While, as we have already noted, there is controversy about the date of the world oil peak, there is virtually no doubt or dispute that it will occur. Moreover, it matters relatively little whether the actual peak arrives this year or in a few years' time, because it will not appear as a sudden, high, isolated pinnacle, but will merely be the highpoint on a gentle curve.[4]

The post-peak decline in supplies need not be catastrophic in itself, as it will probably represent an accumulating shortfall of only about two percent per year, at least for the first decade.[5] However, for a world that is accustomed to relentless expansion in available energy supplies to support growing economic activity and a growing population, the perception that this will be a long, unavoidable, and terminal decline in the energy lifeblood of the modern world may be devastating indeed.

Our Dependence on Oil

It was inevitable that societies would become dependent on oil, once they had developed the technological means to use it, since petroleum provides a concentrated source of energy that is convenient to transport and use, and since it can be transformed into a wide range of useful products—from plastics to clothing to industrial chemicals. Moreover, throughout the last century oil remained extraordinarily cheap in view of its amazing benefits.

Some of the ways we use oil are more apparent than others; the most obvious of all is in *transportation*. We all have direct experience with oil when we fill up the gas tank in our car. We may also know that the jet airplanes that we fly in burn kerosene, another product made from crude oil. Altogether, about 90 percent of the world's transportation relies on oil or oil by-products.

The scale of our transportation systems has exploded over the past century, with per–capita yearly travel distances increasing by 1000 percent from 1900 to 2000.[6] Entire industries (such as airlines, tourism, and highway construction) have grown up, and trade has become globalized—all due to the availability of cheap transportation fuel. As nations rely increasingly on importing manufactured goods from elsewhere, indigenous production falls by the wayside, so that a cutoff in transportation could result in local shortages of wide ranges of products, resources, and services.

But some other uses of oil that are just as essential to modern life are less obvious; the foremost among these is *agriculture*. Conventional industrial agriculture is entirely dependent on fossil fuels. Artificial ammonia-based nitrogenous fertilizers use natural gas and atmospheric nitrogen as raw materials. Much of the world's cropland has been so chemically exhausted, its topsoil so weathered and destroyed that, without these artificial fertilizers (or extensive work to rebuild the topsoil), it cannot produce crops in the volume or at the pace that the world's population now requires. The use of farm machinery impelled by internal-combustion engines, which of course run on petroleum products, has freed up millions of acres of cropland from the need to grow feed for draft animals; those acres now grow food for the burgeoning human population. Without oil, farming may again require animal power, and those animals will need to be fed.

Farms always attract pests; however, the growing of monocrops, which is made economically necessary by mechanization, attracts huge numbers of insect pests. Oil provides the feedstock for making the cheap and effective pesticides required to control these swarms of pests and to maintain crop yields.

In the 1960s, industrial-chemical agricultural practices began to be exported to what was then being called the Third World; this spreading of technologies and fuel use, along with the introduction of more productive crop varieties, was glowingly dubbed the Green Revolution. It enabled a tripling of food production during the ensuing half-century.[7] With the global proliferation of the industrial-chemical agri-

Things Made from Oil

Computer chips • Dishwashing liquids
Paint brushes • Telephones
Unbreakable dishes • Insecticides
Antiseptics • Fishing lures • Deodorant • Tires
Motorcycle helmets • Linoleum • Clothing
Tents • Refrigerator linings • Paint rollers
Floor wax • Shoes • Electrician's tape
Plastic wood • Glue • Roller-skate wheels
Trash bags • Skis • Hand lotion • Clothesline
Dyes • Soft contact lenses • Shampoo
Panty hose • Cameras • Food preservatives
Fishing rods • Oil filters • Transparent tape
Ink • Anesthetics • Upholstery
Disposable diapers • CDs and Cassettes
Mops • House paint • Electric blankets
Awnings • Ammonia • Car battery cases
Safety glass • Hair curlers • Synthetic rubber
Eyeglasses • Vitamin capsules • Movie film
Candles • Rubbing alcohol • Loudspeakers
Credit cards • Fertilizers • Crayons
Insect repellent • Water pipes • Toilet seats
Caulking • Roofing shingles • Balloons
Shower curtains • Garden hose • Golf balls
Umbrellas • Detergents • Milk jugs
Faucet washers • Cold cream • Bandages
Antihistamines • Hair coloring • Nail polish
Guitar strings • False teeth • Yarn
Toothpaste • Golf bags • Tennis rackets
Toothbrushes • Perfume • Luggage
Wire insulation • Shoe polish • Ballpoint pens
Carpeting • Artificial turf • Heart valves
Lipstick • Artificial limbs • Hearing aids
Aspirin • Shaving cream
Wading pools • Parachutes

culture system, the products of that system are now also traded globally, enabling regions to support human populations larger than local resources alone could support. Those systems of global distribution and trade rely on oil.

At the same time, we are extremely dependent on oil as a feedstock for the production of *chemicals and plastics*. Petrochemicals are made by "cracking" oil, a process of breaking hydrocarbon molecules apart with intense heat and sometimes a chemical catalyst; these chemicals are the raw materials for an uncountable number of things both frivolous and essential. Some of the more common petrochemical building blocks of our industrial world are ethylene, propylene, and butadiene. Further processing of just these three chemicals produces products as common, diverse, and important as disinfectants, solvents, antifreezes, coolants, lubricants, heat transfer fluids, and of course plastics.

One of the most important petrochemicals, ethylene, can polymerize into polyethylene, a plastic used to make everything from toys to food containers and furniture. Ethylene can also react with chlorine to produce ethylene chloride, which can then be used to produce vinyl chloride, or its polymerized form, polyvinyl chloride (commonly known as PVC or vinyl), another important plastic. PVC is used in everything from building construction materials to clothing and toys.

In addition, we use oil in many instances for *home heating and electricity generation:* in some parts of the world (and this is most often the case in poorer nations), large proportions of national yearly electricity production come from the burning of oil—even though coal and natural gas are more economical options in regions where these fuels are available in sufficient supply. Even in wealthy nations such as the US, some regions rely primarily on oil for home heating.

Our many structures and machines for transportation; food and goods production and distribution; entertainment; medical technology; construction; and information gathering, processing, and dissemination all run on, are lubricated by, cleaned with, or constructed out of petrochemicals. Without petrochemicals, medical science, information technology, modern cityscapes, and countless other aspects of our modern technology-intensive lifestyles would simply not exist.

In all, oil represents the essence of modern life.

Consequences of Fossil Fuel Use
Nevertheless, there have been substantial and growing costs associated with our increasing reliance on petroleum—including the growing problem of chemical pollution of atmosphere, soil, and water.

Both the useful products and the unintended by-products of oil, coal, and natural gas can act as pollutants. Carbon monoxide, sulfur dioxide, and nitrogen oxides from fossil-fuel combustion can contribute to lung cancer, asthma, and cardiovascular problems in urban populations. Sulfur dioxide and nitrogen oxides contribute to acid rain, damaging the plant life that would otherwise help to clean pollutants from the air. Nitrogenous fertilizers (made mostly from natural gas) flow off fields in great quantities, overloading waterways with nutrients and resulting in massive die-offs of delicate aquatic species. Pesticides, plastics, and chemical components of plastics also make their way into many parts of the natural and built landscapes, causing damage as they go.[8]

Some of best-known pollutants, DDT and polychlorinated biphenyls (PCBs), are endocrine-disrupting petrochemicals that affect reproduction and development. While DDT was in use in the US, and for a number of years after it was banned there, human breast milk in the America had an average concentration of 4000 micrograms of DDT per kilogram of milkfat.[9] Boys in Taiwan exposed to PCBs before birth were born with smaller genitalia and shorter anogenital distance than other boys.[10] Though both DDT and PCBs have been banned by many governments since the 1970s, they are still present in water, air, and soil, and are still in use in some areas of the world.

Other petrochemicals in common use today also display endocrine disruption effects. Bisphenol A (BPA), widely used in the US to make polycarbonate plastics, is an endocrine disruptor widely used in the US. BPA is an estrogen imitator and can disrupt the balance of sex hormones in living things that come in contact with it, including humans. Some scientists have linked amphibian population crashes to the presence of BPA. The chemical bond that polymerizes BPA molecules is unstable and breaks down over time. Water stored in polycarbonate drink bottles can become contaminated with BPA, as can soil and waterways where these plastics have been disposed.[11]

However, of all chemical pollutants issuing from fossil fuels, perhaps none have more worrisome potential consequences than the greenhouse gases carbon dioxide (CO_2) and methane. Burning fossil fuels releases CO_2, which traps heat from the Sun, gradually warming the oceans, the atmosphere, and the Earth's surface. The consequences of this warming effect are likely to be a less stable climate, worse storms, the disruption of agriculture, rising sea levels, and pressure on species to adapt to changing habitat. Carbon dioxide is naturally present in the atmosphere in such small quantities (0.036%) that the massive amounts released through fossil fuel use have already measurably altered the Earth's climate.[12]

Along with many other organizations, the Intergovernmental Panel on Climate Change (IPCC, set up by the UN World Health Organization, the World Meteorological Organization, and the UN Environmental Program) has measured current rates of climate change and predicted future effects. Over the last half of the 20th Century, the IPCC observed higher average temperatures over land areas and an increase in precipitation and storm intensity. The IPCC expects the average surface temperature of the Earth to rise by between 2.5 to 10.4 F (or 1.4 to 5.8 degrees C) between the years 1990 and 2100, a rate of change not seen within the last 10,000 years.[13] The last change of this type, triggered not by flooding the atmosphere with carbon but by natural climatic cycles, occurred about 12,000 years ago, when progressively milder temperatures signaled the gradual end of the last ice age. Ten thousand years is roughly the timescale within which the human species began to settle in villages in large numbers, and developed agriculture, plant and animal domestication, metallurgy, and civilization. Global warming could disrupt this delicate harmony between civilization and climate.

The IPCC and other climate-change organizations have already observed a shift in precipitation patterns along with increasing temperatures, with desert margins growing, some areas flooding unpredictably, and more intense and unpredictable storm events occurring all over the world. Further changes are expected to alter the geography of arable land, lead to unpredictable and violent weather patterns, and alter the geographical distribution of many plant and animal species including disease vectors like mosquitoes. Climate change could thus result in widespread famine, disease, and natural disasters.[14]

Recent studies have tended to show that global climate impacts are appearing more quickly and severely than was predicted only a few years ago. A five-year European study of Antarctic ice cores found that current CO_2 levels are 30 percent higher than at any time in the past 650,000 years, and methane levels 130 percent higher. Moreover, the rates of increase are also extremely high—for CO_2, rates are 200 times faster than anything seen in the ancient past. The study, released in November 2005, also found a "very tight" correlation between CO_2 levels and global temperatures.[15]

Meanwhile Greenland's glaciers, once stable, are now retreating rapidly. Ohio State University's Byrd Polar Research Center has found that the Jakobshavn glacier, one of the major drainage outlets of Greenland's interior ice sheet, is thinning over four times faster than was the case during most of the 20th Century; at the same time, the rate at which the ice moves is accelerating.[16] When the Greenland ice sheet melts entirely, as it is projected to do perhaps before the end of the century, the world's oceans will rise by 20 feet (6.1 meters), drowning coastal cities such as London and New York.

Addicted to Oil

On top of all this, our dependence on oil is itself a problem, because oil is not a resource that renews itself. There is no constant rate of oil extraction that is sustainable over the long run. For the past few decades, in nearly every year we have increased the rate at which we extracted oil. In consequence, economies grew, and we began to build our societies assuming that similar kinds and rates of growth would continue indefinitely.

We designed cities around the automobile and the airplane. We have come to depend on computers, synthetic fibers, and chemicals. The easy availability of cheap oil has engendered expectations of constantly expanding benefits such as these—expectations on which we have founded the integrity of our entire economic system.

Even minor disruptions in the supply of oil can bring quick repercussions, as was shown in Britain in 2000, when a hike in fuel prices resulted in strikes by truckers that nearly brought the nation's economy to a standstill.[17] In the next chapter we will examine in more detail the close links between oil usage and economic growth.

In the past, oil shortages or steep price hikes have been temporary or geographically isolated. Most people have assumed that a global and permanent shortage of petroleum would be a problem for future generations, and that in the meantime alternatives to oil would appear. But investments in energy alternatives (including ethanol, hydrogen, and synthetic liquid transport fuels made from coal or natural gas) have been tentative and the quantities so far available are trivial. In fact, 30 years after the oil shocks of the 1970s, we find ourselves more dependent on petroleum than ever before. And now we must confront the inevitability of the peaking and decline of global oil production.

Peak Oil

The basic concept of Peak Oil is derived from experience: during the past century-and-a-half, all older oil fields have been observed to peak and decline in output. The same has been noted with the collective oil endowment of whole nations. Few doubt that the rate of oil production for the world in total will reach a maximum at some point and then begin its inevitable decline.

For a large region such as a nation, the rate of discovery of oil typically reaches a maximum several decades prior to the production peak. This was the case, for example, in the US, the first important producing country to begin its decline. During the early 20th Century, the US was the world's foremost producer and exporter of oil. Discoveries were dramatic and abundant, but began to fall off sharply after 1930. In 1970, the rate of US oil extraction reached its all-time maximum, and has generally declined since then (though later discoveries in Alaska and the Gulf of Mexico helped moderate that decline). Today the United States imports almost two-thirds of the oil it uses.

Indonesia offers another example of the power of depletion. Exploration there began in the late 19th Century, with early finds providing the basis for the formation of the Royal Dutch Shell Company. Huge discoveries occurred around

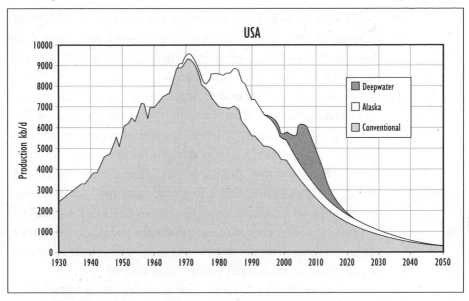

FIGURE 1.1. US oil production, history and projection, including lower 48, Alaska and Gulf of Mexico (deep water). (CREDIT: ASPO.)

1940, and lesser ones in the early 1970s. Production reached a maximum in 1977, slipped, recovered somewhat in the early 90s, and is now in steep decline. Though still a member of the Organization of Petroleum Exporting Countries (OPEC), Indonesia today imports more oil than it exports.

Altogether, according to ChevronTexaco, out of 48 significant oil-producing nations worldwide, 33 are experiencing declining production.[18] In some cases, that decline may be temporarily reversible, but in most instances it will continue inexorably. We don't know exactly when the global peak will happen, but it will almost certainly occur in the early part of this century, and possibly as soon as this year.

Considering the importance of the event, the uncertainty regarding its timing is disturbing. If the peak were to occur within the next five years, national economies would find it impossible to adjust quickly enough (as we will discuss below), while a peak 30 years from now would present a much greater opportunity for adaptation.

We believe, and intend to argue strongly, that leaders and policy makers in both government and industry would be making a fateful mistake by adopting a complacent attitude toward the inevitable world peak of oil production. We see two main reasons for this view: first, that there is strong evidence for concluding that the global peak may occur sooner rather than later; and second, that many years of hard, expensive work will be required to prepare for the peak. Therefore, even if late-peak forecasts prove correct, efforts aimed at mitigating the impacts must begin immediately.

Evidence for a near-term peak includes the fact that global rates of oil discovery have been falling since the early 1960s — as has been confirmed by ExxonMobil.[19] Declining discovery rates represent a well-established trend and cannot be said merely to be the result of transient factors. In 2005 according to IHS Energy Inc., a total of about 5 billion barrels of oil were discovered in new fields — while 31 billion barrels of oil were extracted and used worldwide.[20] Thus, currently only about one barrel of oil is being discovered for every five or six extracted.

Despite this, the global oil industry has been able to replace depleted reserves on a yearly basis until now, mostly by re-estimating the size of existing fields. The Royal Swedish Academy of Sciences, in a recent publication, "Statements on Energy," describes the situation this way:

> In the last 10–15 years, two-thirds of the increases in reserves of conventional oil have been based on increased

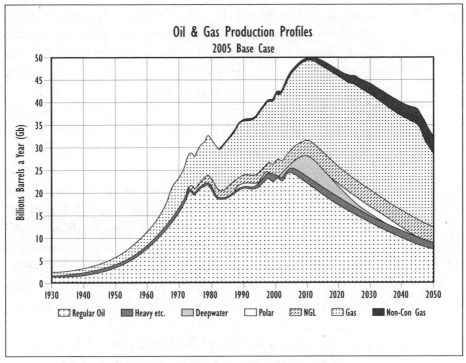

FIGURE 1.2. The general oil and gas depletion picture according to ASPO (CREDIT: ASPO.)

estimates of recovery from existing fields and only one-third on discovery of new fields. In this way, a balance has been achieved between growth in reserves and production. This can't continue. 50% of the present oil production comes from giant fields and very few such fields have been found in recent years.[21]

The 100 or so giant and supergiant fields that are collectively responsible for about half of current world production were all discovered in the 1940s, 50s, 60s, and 70s. Only one or two fields of comparable size have been found since then;

instead, exploration during recent years has turned up a large number of much smaller fields that deplete relatively quickly.

A pivotal report released in 1999 by the United States Geological Survey (USGS), "World Petroleum Assessment 2000," divided its forecasts into "categories of probability"— F95 (which represents a 95 percent chance of at least the amount tabulated), F50 (the median case), F5 (a five percent chance of realization), and Mean (i.e., the arithmetic mean of the estimates). "F" means *fractile*, as defined by the USGS: "Probability (including both geologic and accessibility probabilities) of at least one field equal to or greater than the minimum assessed field size." The USGS F50 and Mean estimates forecast large amounts of oil yet to be discovered and substantial continuing reserve growth for existing fields, yielding a global peak in 2037. However, discoveries from 2000 to the present have not confirmed these expectations; actual discoveries have tended to confirm the report's F95 scenario, which foresees a global production peak in 2016.[22]

Current world oil production stands at 85 million barrels per day, but each year new production capacity must be developed in order both to meet new demand and to offset production rate declines from existing fields-in-production. The International Energy Agency anticipates that new demand added this year will amount to 1.5 Mb/d, while depletion from existing fields will total 4 Mb/d, thus requiring 5.5 Mb/d of new production capacity in order to maintain balance between supply and demand[23] In coming years, incremental demand is projected to grow, as is depletion. How long will the industry be able to keep up on this accelerating treadmill?

Studies attempting to answer this question have come up with contradictory forecasts. Cambridge Energy Research

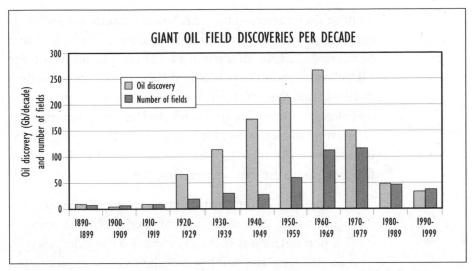

FIGURE 1.3. Giant oil field discoveries by decade. (CREDIT: International Energy Agency, "World Energy Outlook 2004.")

Associates (CERA) in June 2005 issued its "Worldwide Liquids Capacity Outlook to 2010—Tight Supply or Excess of Riches," which identified 16.5 Mb/d of new production capacity that is in development now and that will be brought on line by 2010; the study foresees a need for only about 10 Mb/d or less of new capacity by that time, resulting in a surplus capacity of 6 to 7.5 Mb/d and no global production peak before 2030.[24] However, the Oil Depletion Analysis Centre (ODAC) conducted a parallel survey published in November 2005 which identified a similar list of new production projects, but concluded that supply will fall short of demand as soon as 2007 or 2008, with that inflexion point representing the all-time global production maximum.[25]

How could these two studies have examined the same data and arrived at such different conclusions? Perhaps the most significant factor was the two groups' differing treatment of decline rates. The CERA study assumed a low average decline rate for fields in production; however, Chris Skrebowski, editor of *Petroleum Review* and leader of the ODAC study, notes that "90% of known reserves are in production," and that "as much as 70% of the world's producing oil fields are now in decline" with decline rates averaging between four and six percent per year. Even this figure may be conservative; Andrew Gould, president of the oil services firm Schlumberger, has written that:

> the industry is dealing with a phenomenon that is exaggerated by the lack of investment over the past 18 years. This phenomenon is the decline rate for the older reservoirs that form the backbone of the world's oil production, both in and out of OPEC. An accurate average decline rate is hard to estimate, but an overall figure of 8% is not an unreasonable assumption.[26]

Stuart Staniford, of the online journal www.TheOilDrum .com, has calculated that if Schlumberger's eight percent figure is accurate, global oil production probably cannot increase much above its current level and will begin its decline within the next year or two.[27]

Will new technology increase recovery rates? The "late peakers" assume that it will do so dramatically. However, a recent paper by John Gowdy and Roxana Juliá titled "Technology and Petroleum Exhaustion: Evidence from Two Mega-Oilfields" reaches the conclusion that "Patterns of depletion in these two fields suggest that when a resource is finite, technological improvements do increase supply temporarily. But in these two fields, the effect of new technology was to increase the rate of depletion without altering the fields' ultimate recovery." Further, "Our results imply that temporary low prices may be misleading indicators of future resource scarcity and call into question the future ability of current mega-oilfields to meet a sharp increase in oil demand."[28]

If decline rates, future discovery, the effects of technology, and future reserve growth are all sources of uncertainty in our efforts to assess when the global oil peak will occur, proven petroleum reserve figures are yet another. On the surface, the reserves numbers look reassuring: the world has roughly a trillion barrels yet to produce, perhaps more. Indeed, official reserves figures have never been higher. However, circumstantial evidence suggests that some of the largest producing nations may have inflated their reserves figures for political reasons.[29] Meanwhile oil companies routinely and legitimately report reserve growth for fields discovered decades ago in a practice mandated by the Securities and Exchange Commission that tends to obscure declining discovery rates.[30] In addition, reserves figures are often muddied by the inclusion of non-conventional petroleum resources, such as extra-heavy oil—which do need to be taken into account, but in a separate category, as their rates of extraction are limited by factors different from those that constrain the production of conventional crude.[31] As a consequence of all of these practices, oil reserves data tend to give an impression of expansion and plenty, while discovery and depletion data do the opposite.

All of these uncertainties in the data conspire to invite disagreement among experts as to when the global oil peak will occur. While the US Department of Energy predicts that world oil production will increase over the next 20 years from 85 Mb/d to 119.2 Mb/d to meet anticipated demand,[32] a growing chorus of petroleum geologists and other energy analysts warns that such levels of production may never be seen and that the global peak could occur within months or years.

Among those cautionary voices is that of James Schlesinger, who served as CIA director in the Nixon administration, defense secretary in the Nixon and Ford administrations, and energy secretary in the Carter administration. In November 2005 testimony before the US Senate Foreign Relations Committee, Schlesinger urged lawmakers to begin preparing for declining oil supplies and increasing prices in the coming decades. "We are faced with the possibility of a major economic shock and the political unrest that would ensue," he said.[33]

A French report from the Economics, Industry & Finance Ministry, "The Oil Industry 2004," released in that year, takes a careful look at future production and supply issues, forecasting a possible peak in world production as early as 2013.[34]

Ford Motor Company executive vice president Mark Fields, in his keynote address at the 2005 Society of Automotive Engineers' "Global Leadership Conference at the Greenbrier," noted the seven most serious challenges to his industry, one of which was that "oil production is peaking."[35] Volvo motor company has for several years acknowledged in its company literature that a global oil production peak is likely by 2015.[36]

Legendary petroleum magnate T. Boone Pickens, who co-founded Mesa Petroleum and Petroleum Exploration and now manages $2.5 billion in investments as chairman of BP Capital Management, told the 11th National Clean Cities conference in May 2005 that, "Global oil [production] is 84 million barrels [a day]. I don't believe you can get it any more than 84 million barrels. . . . I think they are on decline in the biggest oil fields in the world today and I know what it's like once you turn the corner and start declining, it's a treadmill that you just can't keep up with."[37]

Royal Dutch Shell chief executive Jeroen Van Der Veer has said that "My view is that 'easy' oil has probably passed its peak."[38]

J. Robinson West, founder and chairman of PFC Energy, one of Washington's most influential international energy consulting firms, is a former Assistant Secretary of the Interior in the Reagan Administration and a member of the advisory council of The National Interest. West predicts that the "tipping point" when global supply of oil ceases to grow could arrive in 2015.[39]

Veteran petroleum geologist Henry Groppe, a Houston-based independent analyst who began his career in 1945 and who is today a consultant to global corporations as well as to nations, said in 2005 that "Total crude oil production may have peaked this year, or perhaps will peak next year." Over the short term (until 2010 or so) Groppe foresees shortfalls being cushioned by an increase in production of natural gas liquids, and by a switch, among developing nations, from oil-fired power plants to coal-fired boilers.[40]

Matthew Simmons, founder of Simmons & Company international energy investment bank, has been perhaps the most outspoken of oil analysts and investors regarding Peak Oil. He is the author of *Twilight in the Desert: The Coming Saudi Oil Shock and the World Economy* (Wiley, 2005). Simmons has concluded, on the basis of his study of technical papers from the Society of Petroleum Engineers, that Saudi Arabian oil production could be close to its maximum, and that world oil production is also therefore close to its peak.

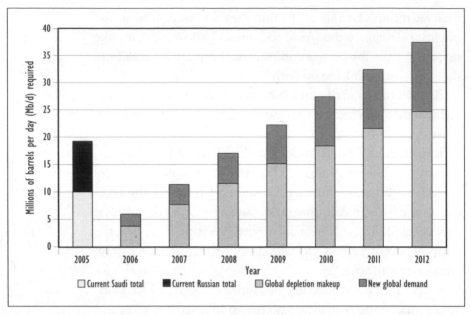

FIGURE 1.4. Cumulative new production capacity (each year's total including the previous year's) required to meet new demand and to offset declines in production from existing fields. For comparison, 2005 production totals from the two largest producers, Saudi Arabia and Russia, are indicated in the first column. (CREDIT: International Energy Agency data compiled in graphic form by Moshe Braner.)

Other prominent individuals who have publicly stated their concerns about Peak Oil include politicians from many nations (such as French National Assembly member Yves Cochet, British Member of Parliament Michael Meacher, and US Representative Roscoe Bartlett), journalists (such as BBC's Adam Porter and *The Guardian's* George Monbiot), and economists (Richard Douthwaite of FEASTA and James Hamilton of the University of California, San Diego), among many others.

On March 1, 2006 the *New York Times* published on its website an editorial by Robert Semple, Associate Editor of the Editorial Page for the *Times* since 1998, in which he wrote, "The concept of peak oil has not been widely written about. But people are talking about it now. It deserves a careful look—largely because it is almost certainly correct."[41]

It is of course a simple matter to produce an equally impressive list of institutions (USGS, the US Department of Energy, IEA, CERA, and ExxonMobil) and individuals (Pulitzer Prize winner Daniel Yergin and oil industry analyst Michael Lynch) who have concluded that the peak of global production will not occur before 2025 at the earliest, and that it is an event we should therefore not be concerned about today.

Studies suggesting peak dates:
Kenneth Deffeyes 2005[42]
Henry Groppe 2006[43]
Ali Samsam Bakhtiari 2007[44]
Richard Duncan 2007[45]
ODAC 2007[46]
Colin Campbell 2010[47]
Rembrandt Koppelaar 2013[48]
Jean Laherrere 2015[49]
PFC Energy 2015[50]
CERA after 2020[51]
USGS after 2030[52]

For the policy maker, this lack of agreement among experts and official agencies presents a dilemma. Responding to Peak Oil will require intense, sustained effort and enormous investment. Why put forth that effort, and why shift scarce investment capital away from other priorities, when it is not even clear that future global oil supplies present a problem? Doesn't it make sense to wait until the experts reach a consensus, or until events make the need for action unavoidably clear?

The Danger of Assuming an Easy Fix

It is important to resolve the controversy over whether global oil production will peak in 2006 or 2035. However, absolute certainty regarding the timing of Peak Oil will be attainable only after the fact. Meanwhile, we must speak in terms of probabilities and risks.

It would appear, from uncertainty in the data, that a near-term peak in production cannot be ruled out. If, as we propose to show, the consequences of peaking soon are likely to be profound, then even a relatively low likelihood of occurrence should be treated with utmost seriousness. After all, by way of analogy, few of us would be so foolish as to leave a company, a city, or even a house exposed to the risks of fire and accident liability without insurance. And unlike a house fire or other accident or natural disaster, the risk of a peak in world oil production grows every day as we deplete the resource.

How severe are the consequences of Peak Oil likely to be? What will be the challenges of offsetting those consequences? And how much time will be required in order to pursue mitigation strategies?

These questions have all been addressed in an important study, "The Peaking of World Oil Production: Impacts, Mitigation and Risk Management," prepared by Science Applications International (SAIC) for the US Department of Energy, released in February 2005. The project leader for the study was Robert L. Hirsch, who has had a distinguished career in formulating energy policy. The report on the study will hereinafter be referred to as "The Hirsch Report."

The first paragraph of the Hirsch Report's Executive Summary states:

> The peaking of world oil production presents the U.S. and the world with an unprecedented risk management problem. As peaking is approached, liquid fuel prices and price volatility will increase dramatically, and, without timely mitigation, the economic, social, and political costs will be unprecedented. Viable mitigation options exist on both the supply and demand sides, but to have substantial

impact, they must be initiated more than a decade in advance of peaking.[53]

As the Hirsch Report explains in detail, due to our systemic dependence on oil for transportation, agriculture, and the production of plastics and chemicals, every sector of every society will be affected. Efforts will be needed to create alternative sources of energy, to reduce demand for oil through heightened energy efficiency, and, by implication, to redesign entire systems (including cities) to operate with less petroleum.

The study's methodology involved the examination of three scenarios:

- Scenario I assumed that action is not initiated until peaking occurs.
- Scenario II assumed that action is initiated 10 years before peaking.
- Scenario III assumed action is initiated 20 years before peaking.

In all three scenarios, the Hirsch Report assumes a "crash program" scale of effort (that is, all the resources of government and industry are marshalled to the task). The Report concludes that, due to the time required to start efforts and the scale of mitigation required, no preparation will result in at least 20 years of fuel shortfalls. With 10 years of preparation, a minimal 10-year shortfall is likely. And with 20 years of advance mitigation effort, there is "the possibility" of averting fuel shortages altogether. The Report also concludes that "Early mitigation will almost certainly be less expensive

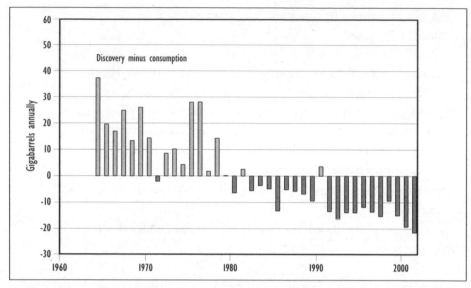

FIGURE 1.5A. Discovery minus consumption: prior to 1980, more new oil was discovered yearly than was extracted; since then, more has been extracted yearly than has been discovered. (CREDIT: ASPO.)

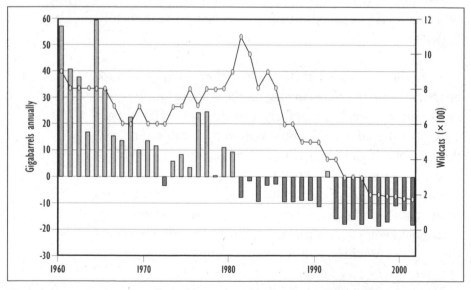

FIGURE 1.5B. Exploration efforts during the 1980s versus net amounts discovered, minus amounts consumed. Increasing rates of drilling yielded little in the way of new oil. (CREDIT: ASPO.)

than delayed mitigation," and that therefore the costs of preparing too late for Peak Oil will be far greater than those of preparing too soon.

In other words, if global Peak Oil is 20 years away or fewer, *or we believe it might be*, then we must begin immediately with a full-scale effort to address the problem.

The Hirsch Report effectively undermines the standard free-market argument that oil depletion poses no serious problem, now or later, because as oil becomes scarcer the price will rise until demand is reduced commensurate with supply, with higher prices stimulating more exploration, the development of alternative fuels, and more efficient use of remaining quantities. While it is true that rising prices will do all of these things, we have no assurance that the effects will be sufficient or timely enough to avert severe, protracted economic, social, and political disruptions.

First, price increases may or may not stimulate more exploration, or do so sufficiently or productively. During most of the 20th Century, more exploration resulted in more oil found. However, in recent decades, exploration efforts have turned up fewer and fewer finds. During the 1980s, as discoveries declined, companies responded by spending more on exploration, but their increasing investments did not result in more oil found (see Fig 1.5a-b). During the years 2002 through 2004 the global oil industry spent roughly 8 billion dollars per year on exploration, but found, on average, less than 4 billion dollars' worth of oil each year (see Fig 1.6).

Higher prices for oil will also no doubt spur new investment in alternative fuels. But the time required to gain the ability to produce substantial quantities of alternative fuels will be considerable, given the volume of our global transportation fuel consumption. Moreover the amount of in-

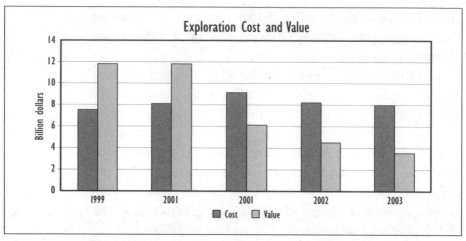

FIGURE 1.6. In recent years, the cost of exploration for oil has been exceeding the net present value of the discoveries in absolute terms. In simple terms, these days it usually costs more to explore for oil than consequent oil discoveries warrant. This trend appears to be accelerating. (CREDIT: ASPO.)

vestment required will be immense. And in some cases the inherent problem of scale is independent of time or money: it would simply be unrealistic to expect some alternatives to fully or even substantially replace oil at any level of investment, and even with decades of work.

Let us examine a few of the most often-cited candidates.

The world possesses enough coal to last many decades or even centuries at current rates of usage, and technology already exists to turn coal into a high-quality petroleum liquid.[54] The most advanced available process involves gasifying the coal, removing impurities from the gas, and then synthesizing liquids from it by way of the Fisher-Tropsch process. About 150 gasifiers are already in use around the world, and the largest existing coal-to-liquids (CTL) facilities are plants operated by Sasol Corporation in South Africa. Those plants currently produce about 150,000 barrels of synthetic oil per day. China is currently investing $6 billion in production facilities that will make 14 million barrels of oil equivalent per year. (At this rate, the cost to replace the entire 30 billion barrels per year of total world petroleum usage would be nearly $13 trillion.) The time needed to build a CTL plant and pay back the initial investment is estimated to be between 5 and 8 years.[55] The inherent costliness of the CTL process is understandable from the standpoint of energy accounting: coal starts out as a fuel that is substantially less energy-dense than oil; then, about 40 percent of the coal energy is lost in the conversion process. Thus larger scales of production are unlikely to bring down the cost substantially. The very considerable environmental impacts of increasing our global usage of coal could be somewhat offset by carbon sequestration technology,[56] but this would add to the energy cost of liquids production and therefore also to the monetary cost of the finished product.

Similar technology exists to turn natural gas into synthetic petroleum liquids. Gas-to-liquids (GTL) is a cleaner process from an environmental point of view, and is also less capital intensive than CTL. However, natural gas prices are currently higher than those for coal, and some regions of the world do not have access to natural gas. Shell currently operates a GTL plant in Malaysia producing 14,500 b/d, and several other large commercial plants are planned, including three large units in Qatar—a 140,000 b/d facility operated by Shell, a 160,000 b/d ConocoPhillips facility, and a 120,000 b/d Marathon Oil plant. The total output from projects under development and consideration is projected to be roughly 1.7 Mb/d, but not all will come to fruition. Given the current investment environment, the Hirsch Report estimates that 1.0 Mb/d of capacity may be installed by 2015.[57] In other words, without sharply accelerated investment (on the scale of hundreds of billions or trillions of dollars), GTL will contribute in only a minor way to reducing our dependence on conventional oil.

The current world production of biofuels (ethanol, wood methanol, and biodiesel) represents a tiny fraction of the volume of liquid fuels from petroleum. The world produces (with the help of fossil fuels) more vegetable oil than is consumed as food or in industrial applications, and a study by Environment Canada[58] estimates that this surplus oil could produce between three and five million tons[59] of biodiesel per year with current technology. Biodiesel can be made from rape seed, palm, soy, and other oil crops. Methanol can be made from biomass, as well as from natural gas or coal. Ethanol can make use of otherwise undervalued waste biomass, and is useful for converting relatively low-quality solid fuels into high-quality liquid fuel.[60] Ethanol contains about 75 percent of the energy of gasoline per gallon, compared to 67 percent for methanol; biodiesel contains roughly as much energy per gallon as gasoline or slightly more.[61] The major drawbacks of biofuels are their land and input requirements. For example, to meet the diesel demands of Washington State exclusively with biodiesel would require more cropland than exists in the entire state.[62] An analysis by Ted Trainer of research by Berndes, Hoogwijk and van den Broek[63] concludes that:

> Total global biomass growth is far below present global energy use, and liquid plus gas use. The proportion of this growth that could be harvested would be a small proportion of the total, and from this energy costs would have to

be deducted. In other words there would seem to be no possibility that world biomass can meet more than a quite small proportion of present world liquid plus gas fuel demand.[64]

The idea of a "hydrogen economy" has elicited considerable discussion in recent years. The idea is essentially to use hydrogen as an energy storage medium to power vehicles. Surplus electricity produced during off-peak hours, and especially from variable renewable sources such as wind and sun, could be used to produce hydrogen from water by electrolysis; the hydrogen could then be processed through fuel cells to produce electricity once more. There would be no carbon emissions or other pollution released in the burning of hydrogen fuel. Unfortunately, however, most analysts agree that, even assuming robust investment, a hydrogen economy is decades away.[65]

Standard economic theory holds that the increased cost of oil should also spur conservation and efficiency. Again, however, theory may seriously underestimate the time and investment needed.

An obvious example: the world's fleet of automobiles and trucks could be made much more fuel-efficient, and this would cut a substantial amount of the current demand for oil as a transportation fuel. This is particularly true in the nation with the largest number of vehicles, the United States, where fleet fuel efficiency for cars is quite low, about 22 miles per gallon (10.7 liters/100 km).[66] Technology exists (including electric/ICE hybrid engines, diesel hybrids, and plug-in hybrids) that could easily achieve between 60 and 100 mpg (3.9 to 2.4 liters/100 km) per vehicle. However, auto manufacturers would require at least five years for retooling in order to produce the new high-efficiency vehicles in large numbers. Then, since not everyone buys a new car every year, there would be a time lag involved in fleet replacement: roughly 15 years would be required for the majority of existing cars and trucks to be traded in for newer energy-efficient models. Altogether, then, 20 years would be needed for the full implementation of this strategy.

Thus Peak Oil will present problems on nearly every front whose solutions will take considerable time and immense amounts of investment capital. We do not mean to suggest that there are no answers to these problems, only that the problems will not disappear automatically due to the working of markets, since price signals accompanying declining oil production will come too late to be of much help. Moreover, as the Hirsch Report emphasizes, these problems' solutions will require the participation of both government and the private sector.

The Oil Depletion Protocol

Mitigation efforts will be challenging enough in the context of a stable economic environment. However, if prices for oil become extremely volatile, mitigation and transition programs could be made more difficult or undermined altogether. While high but stable prices would encourage conservation and investment in alternatives, prices that repeatedly skyrocket and then plummet could devastate entire economies and discourage long-term planning and investment. Those nations, and those aspects of national economies, that could not obtain oil at any price they could afford would suffer the worst impacts. Supply interruptions would likely occur with greater frequency and for increasing lengths of time as global oil production gradually waned.

Meanwhile the perception among importers that exporting nations were profiteering would foment animosities and an escalating likelihood of international and internal conflicts. We will discuss this in the next chapter.

In short, the global peak in oil production is likely to lead to economic chaos and extreme geopolitical tensions, raising the spectres of war, revolution, terrorism, and even famine, unless nations adopt some method of cooperatively reducing their reliance on oil.

This book is primarily about one such proposed method —perhaps the simplest imaginable. Under an Oil Depletion Protocol nations would agree to reduce their oil production and oil imports according to a consistent, sensible formula. This would have two principal effects: first, it would reduce price volatility and enable nations, municipalities, industries, and companies to plan their economic future; and second, it would reduce international competition for remaining oil resources.

The problem we are facing—the depletion of a vital resource—is one that we as a species have never encountered before on such a vast scale, and it is an extremely serious one. And the proposed strategy for addressing it—in effect, a global rationing system—while straightforward enough to be stated on a single page, is in some respects unprecedented and its implications are not obvious; it therefore requires some justification and explanation, along with a discussion of possible alternatives.

The Oil Depletion Protocol will not by itself solve all of the problems raised by Peak Oil. But it should make those problems much easier to address, providing a context of global agreement in which the task of energy transition can be planned and supported over the long term—a context, that is, of stable energy prices and peaceful cooperation.

2

Without a Protocol:

A Century of Chaos?

W E HOPE ALREADY TO HAVE SHOWN that a good argument can be made for the Oil Depletion Protocol.
However, the Protocol is an essentially restrictive measure,
and, given all nations' preference for continued economic expansion (which usually implies growth in energy usage), this
agreement is unlikely to be readily accepted *unless it is understood to be preferable to economic, social, or geopolitical harms* that
would far outweigh the pain or inconvenience of foregoing
the portion of conventional economic growth based on the
increased use of oil. Calculations of costs versus benefits-
from-harm-avoidance are inherent in most regulations—
which are by their very nature restrictive (and therefore costly
to someone), but regulations are often accepted in any case
because they are seen as necessary to the prevention of even
more costly problems later.

So to properly make the case for the global Oil Depletion
Protocol, it is necessary to set forth a more detailed picture of
what will likely happen if the Protocol is not adopted. This

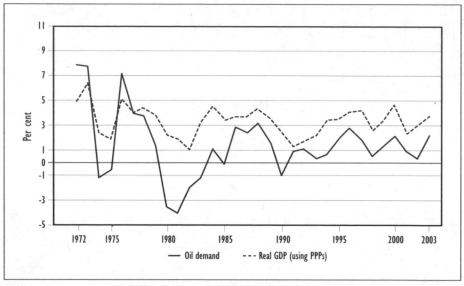

FIGURE 2.1. Relationship between Oil Demand and GDP Growth. Except during the 1970s and 1980s, when most of the world's nuclear power plants come into operation and reduced the demand for oil to fuel electricity generation, there is clearly a strong correlation. When many countries ceased adopting more nuclear power, oil demand accordingly grew by about two percent to deliver the required growth of GDP. (CREDIT: International Energy Agency, "World Energy Outlook 2004.")

effort will fail if our picture is unrealistic or exaggerated in any way, and so we have sought to describe consequences conservatively.

The Global Economy

Without the Protocol, as oil production declines prices will almost certainly rise, though probably in unpredictable increments. Prices will become more volatile. It is just as clear that uncontrollably and unpredictably rising oil costs (and energy costs in general) will damage the global economy. But how much and in what ways?

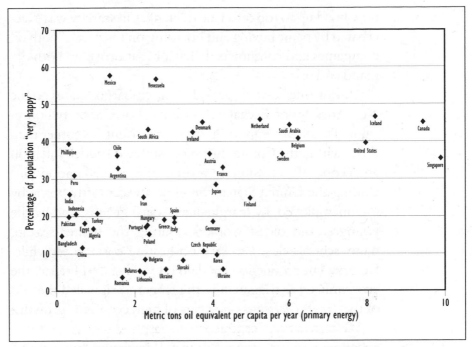

FIGURE 2.2. How self-reported levels of happiness vary according to per-capita energy consumption in various nations. (CREDIT: Data from BP, World Values Survey, and the UN, put in graphic form by Nathan John Hagens.)

We can perhaps begin to answer these questions by examining past instances of steeply rising oil prices — of which the most dramatic were the oil shocks of the 1970s.

The 1973 Arab OPEC oil embargo produced economic chaos in the West. The price of oil shot up from US$2.90 per barrel in mid-1973 to US$11.65 in December of that year, raising the price of many other goods. In the US, the retail price of a gallon of gasoline rose from an average of 38.5 cents in May 1973 to 55.1 cents in June 1974. Uncertainty as to the reliability of supply changed buying habits, as drivers who would previously have cruised happily on a quarter of a tank now lined up to top off a half-full tank. Oil scarcity was exacerbated by panic buying and hoarding on the part of both oil companies and consumers, behavior that drove up both demand and price.

During one six-week period of the embargo, shares on the New York Stock Exchange lost a total of US$97 billion in value. Petroleum-importing industrial countries (other than those within the Communist bloc) suffered sudden inflation and economic recession. In most of the affected nations, including the United States, the impact was mostly borne by the unemployed, by marginalized social groups, and by the youngest and oldest workers. During the winter season, many schools closed to save on heating costs; meanwhile, factories cut production and laid off workers. In France, the economic crisis triggered by the embargo signalled the end of the *Trente Glorieuses* — 30 years of high economic growth.[1]

Western nations' central banks sharply cut interest rates to encourage growth; the result was a persisting "stagflation" that crippled economies for years. Many economists regard the period of the oil shocks of the 1970s as the worst global economic crisis since the Great Depression.

Will future energy crises follow a similar pattern? Of course it is impossible to know. However, according to a recent article in the *Financial Times,* the International Monetary Fund is already worried about the impact of high oil prices:

> The IMF estimates that oil prices explain half of the deterioration of the US current account deficit between 2002 and 2005. In that period, the deficit rose 2 percentage points, to a record 6.5 per cent of gross domestic product. Rodrigo Rato, IMF managing director, this week warned

that "good economic performance rests on a shaky foundation, because of large and continuing global imbalances." The US current account deficit is forecast to increase again in 2006, Mr Rato said, partly because of the impact of high energy prices.

According to the article, Mr. Rato has called for a "multilateral" resolution to the imbalances, warning that the "risk is that global imbalances will be unwound in an abrupt and disorderly way."[2]

In some respects, many nations today appear better prepared to resist the effects of high oil prices: their economies now use oil more efficiently, and oil costs represent a smaller fraction of their GDP. However, even though some nations use oil more efficiently than they did 30 years ago, having less oil available each year might still be extremely damaging to their economies if oil is just as important to the goods and services required. In fact, shortages or sharp price hikes might actually hurt more, given the fact that easy efficiency gains have already been made. Further increases in efficiency may be costly and may require time to implement. Moreover, the shortages of the 1970s were temporary and political in origin, whereas Peak Oil implies shortages that are imposed by nature and are ongoing and cumulative.

The Hirsch Report predicts, for industrialized nations:

> ...increased costs for the production of goods and services, as well as inflation, unemployment, reduced demand for products other than oil, and lower capital investment. Tax revenues decline and budget deficits increase, driving up interest rates. These effects will be greater the more abrupt and severe the oil price increase

and will be exacerbated by the impact on consumer and business confidence.[3]

Elsewhere, the Report's authors note that:

> Higher oil price volatility can lead to reduction in invest-
> ment in other parts of the economy, leading in turn to a
> long-term reduction in supply of various goods, higher
> prices, and further reduced macroeconomic activity. In-
> creasing volatility has the potential to increase both eco-
> nomic disruption and transaction costs for both con-
> sumers and producers, adding to inflation and reducing
> economic growth rates.[4]

The Hirsch Report also concludes that, in the post-peak economic environment, less-industrialized nations "will likely be even worse off." A recent study by Karim Jaufeerally on the likely impacts to one small less-industrialized country, Mauritius, noted that with oil prices "at US $110 per barrel...the Mauritian economy will be in severe trouble."[5]

One of the most significant world economic developments since the 1970s has been the globalization of trade, a trend that Peak Oil may reverse, at least to some extent. According to a recent paper by economists Jeff Rubin and Benjamin Tal at the Canadian Imperial Bank of Commerce (CIBC), as oil prices raise shipping costs North American retailers will find goods from Asia—such as apparel, furniture, footwear, metal goods, textiles, and industrial machinery—less attractive. Overall transport costs will be about 130 per cent higher with oil at US$100 than at US$30 a barrel, according to the report. "All of a sudden," the economists write, "proximity to major markets becomes far more important in determining comparative advantage. Distance translates directly into costs."[6]

If oil prices rise rapidly, companies will find it difficult to pass their higher costs along to buyers quickly enough to offset their own losses. Larger companies with big inventories will be able to afford to put off price hikes longer, so smaller producers will be hit harder. When retail prices for manufactured goods do go up, they will tend to suppress demand, so producers will be hit both ways: their costs will balloon while their volume of sales shrinks. The end result may be a consolidation of many industries, leaving only a few large companies in place.

Secondary economic impacts, caused by the interaction of high oil prices with unrelated problems having to do with currency values, financial derivatives, or debt bubbles, are more difficult to predict with any assurance, but could be profound.

Transportation

Transportation as a whole (including freight) currently accounts for over 60 percent of all oil consumed globally; conversely, the world's transportation systems are over 90 percent dependent on petroleum.

Increases in oil prices will not affect all transportation modes equally. The energy intensity of transport by rail, ship, truck, car, and plane is quite varied, with transport by plane the most energy-intensive, followed in order by car, truck, rail, and ship. Altogether, the transport of goods by plane is up to 25 times more energy-intensive than transport by ship.[7]

Personal/Local Transportation
The most familiar, easily observable role of oil in daily life, at least for people living in the industrialized world, is as a fuel for personal transportation. When the price of oil rises, people feel the direct impact at the gas pump, with the most ob-

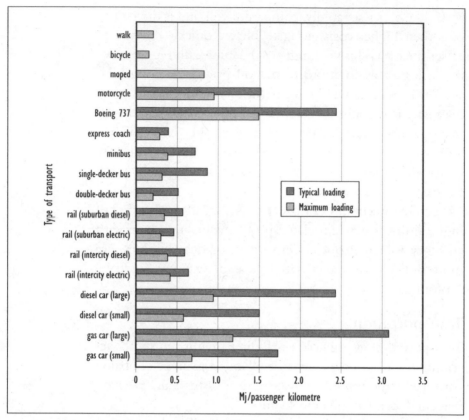

FIGURE 2.3.   Energy efficiency of various modes of passenger transport in the UK.
(CREDIT: http://www.open.ac.uk/T206/illustrations/figure1_49.htm.)

vious effect of high oil prices being more and louder grum-
bling about the cost of daily commutes. But, because transportation of people and goods is so vital to economic activity
and because transportation is so oil-intensive, high oil prices
generate many more problems than commuter disgruntle-
ment.

Many modern cities, suburbs, and towns have been designed in such a way as to require the use of motorized trans-

port. Especially for residents of suburbs or rural areas, a personal car has become a vital tool for getting to and from sources of employment, education, socialization, food, clothing, and medicine.

Since most households now have two workers instead of one, living close to the sites of both jobs is often not possible in the standard suburban setting, and therefore many workers commute long distances to the workplace. Two workers traveling to two separate workplaces require two separate cars. With two cars, there is more opportunity, for example, for one partner to take a two-mile detour to rent a movie for the evening while the other detours to the mall to pick up groceries. With more workers per household, travel for all reasons has increased.

The prevalence of single-occupant vehicles on the commute to work seems roughly to correlate with city sprawl.[8] At the same time, public transit ridership seems roughly to correlate with city density, particularly for more populous cities.[9]

The working poor are more careful with transportation dollars and transportation energy than more affluent suburbanites. They spend, on average, far less than middle- and upper-class workers on transportation. However, if expenditures on transportation are taken as a percentage of income, poor workers spend considerably more of their incomes on transportation than other workers, especially where they use a personal car. Thus the working poor are more reliant on cheap fuel for the maintenance of their income-and-expense balance than are the more monied classes. Given a full range of options, the working poor tend disproportionately to use alternative forms of transportation, such as public transit, carpooling, bicycling, and walking.[10] But with many poor

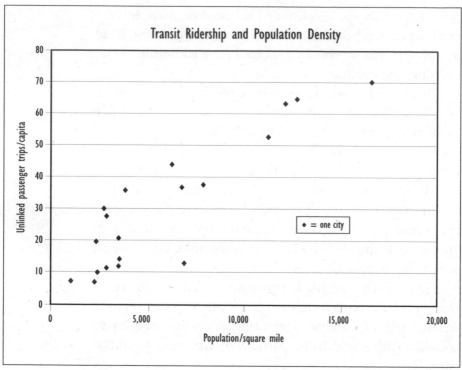

FIGURE 2.4. How public transit ridership varies according to population density in the top 19 US cities over 50,000, excluding New York. (CREDIT: Data from US Census Bureau put in graphic form by Jennifer Bresee.)

communities pushed out of core urban centers due to gentrification, alternative transportation options are not always available.

Oil demand is only somewhat elastic. As with demand for food or water, high prices can suppress demand for energy only so far. After suburbanites cut back on fuel use by curtailing frivolous trips, whatever trips remain are essential, and unless settlement patterns are radically altered (a project requiring years of planning and expensive effort), many people

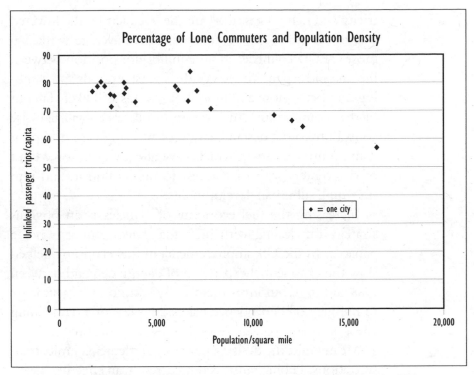

FIGURE 2.5.   Percentage of lone commuters in selected US cities from the 50 largest metropolitan areas, excluding New York. (CREDIT: Data from the US Census Bureau put in graphic form by Jennifer Bresee.)

will still need to make these essential trips with cars. Thus the design of settlements creates a low threshold of fuel costliness that cannot be crossed without severely damaging the economy as a whole.

The cost of gasoline, when adjusted for inflation or other skewing factors, fell steadily between 1983 and 2001. While the cost of fuel drifted lower, the cost of other goods rose, taking a larger percentage of consumers' budgets. Thus the cost of other goods, and of other types of energy such as electricity and natural gas, took up the slack left by the lowered cost of oil and in general maintained the average worker in most OECD countries in an equilibrium position between income and expenditures.[11] With expensive goods and climbing oil prices, more and more households will likely fall out of that equilibrium. An increase in oil prices will likewise contribute to the destabilization of working-class and poor communities, many of which have already been forced out of city centers with easy access to public transit, and into sprawling suburban developments.

Increasing the fuel economy of vehicles is an obvious strategy for dealing with high fuel prices, but it is not a panacea. In the US, improvements in fuel economy helped slow the exponential expansion of energy demand between 1988 and 1991, but investment in fuel economy as a strategy to mitigate oil dependence has had far less of a dampening effect on energy consumption from 1991 to the present.

Meanwhile, the design of existing settlements limits transit options. Public transit is not currently an effective means of transportation in localities characterized by urban sprawl: efficient, cost-effective public transit requires hubs of activity around which to build a network of transit connections, and sprawling settlements lack such hubs.

Public transit ridership seems broadly to grow and shrink with fuel availability, and also seems to grow and shrink with national economic health. Where public transit does exist in suburban areas, it typically consists of buses. However, buses are the least efficient of all public transit modes. A bus filled with passengers uses 84 percent as much fuel as those passengers would collectively use to go the same distance in private vehicles. Commuter rail uses 31 percent as much fuel as the equivalent number of single-occupant vehicles, light rail 22 percent as much, and heavy rail only 17 percent as much.[12] Like private commuters, public transit systems are vulnerable to oil price increases.

Trucking/Other Freight

With higher fuel prices the extra cost of shipping goods will ultimately be added to the price of the goods. Currently freight companies, particularly trucking companies, are suffering financially while the price of shipping comes into balance with the price of fuel. In the US alone, each one-cent increase in the price per gallon (3.8 liters) of diesel fuel translates to a US$350,000,000 increase in costs per year to the trucking industry.[13] Many trucking companies have added a fuel surcharge to their commercial deliveries, but that surcharge often does not cover all of the added cost of fuel for the shipment.

Many industries and retailers are currently feeling the pinch of high freight charges due to high fuel prices, but have managed to absorb much of the added cost internally, passing only a fraction of the cost on to customers. For a typical retail product, the producer may sell to a distributor at a price that reflects only a modest added cost resulting from oil price increases (unless the product incorporates oil in its production, in which case the product becomes more expensive). The global and/or national distributor then sells to regional hubs at an added cost (the fuel surcharge) on top of that, but the added charge may only cover part of the added cost from recent fuel price hikes. The regional distributors then sell to retailers at another added cost (another fuel surcharge) on top of the previous markup, but again one that may not entirely cover the actual extra cost of fuel. The retailer sells to customers and tacks on another added cost, but one that, yet again, usually does not completely cover the added cost of fuel. Every party in the distribution network, from the global level to the corner store to the customer, pays higher prices and absorbs higher costs due to high fuel prices. Often, long-term contracts keep the prices of goods fixed for a number of years. Fuel surcharges that translate into higher costs to workers and shareholders, rather than high price increases passed directly to the customer, are the immediate symptom of petroleum shortage.

Some vital businesses, such as supermarkets, have such thin margins for profitability that they cannot absorb these added costs while maintaining normal levels of service. Supermarkets will have to either pass the added costs on to customers or drastically change their business models to take advantage of local resources if they wish to remain profitable. Food in general, and particularly perishable goods that have to be shipped within a certain timeframe—such as milk, meat, and produce—will likely become much more expensive in response to high fuel prices. Goods that require petroleum in their manufacture as well as distribution—such as tires, chemicals, and plastic products—will also likely cost proportionally more. Thus high fuel prices threaten the availability and affordability of nearly all goods used in modern life, save those produced locally and without the use of petroleum, and will particularly impact the price and availability of essentials like food.

Air Transport

Commercial airlines have been facing a crisis in profitability for years. Among the many challenges the industry faces is rising fuel costs. Fuel is the second largest cost involved in air transport, both passenger and shipping, after labor. For passenger airlines, a one-cent increase in the price of a gallon (3.8 liters) of jet fuel leads to an extra cost of one million dollars per year, and a one-dollar increase in crude oil prices per barrel leads to an extra cost of $50 million per year.[14]

Airfares have not risen substantially in recent years despite increases in fuel costs, because customers have not been willing to fly with higher fares—given other high-profile risks associated with the air travel industry, such as terrorism. But the price of air transportation will inevitably increase, since airlines need a certain baseline level of funds to maintain their fleets and pay workers. Before the price of air travel comes in balance with fuel cost, more commercial air carriers will likely file for bankruptcy, and in the end air freight and commercial air travel will become much more expensive.

Food and Agriculture

Recent and current trends in global food production are closely related to the increased use of inexpensive fossil fuels.

Arable Cropland

For millennia, the total amount of arable cropland gradually increased due to the clearing of forests and the irrigation of land that would otherwise be too arid for cultivation. That amount has reached a maximum within the past two decades and is now decreasing because of the salinization of irrigated soils and the relentless growth of cities, with their buildings, roads, and parking lots. Irrigation has become more widespread because of the availability of cheap energy to operate pumps, while urbanization is largely a result of cheap fuel-fed transportation and the flushing of the peasantry from the countryside as a consequence of their inability to buy or to compete with fuel-fed agricultural machinery.

Topsoil

The world's existing soils were generated over thousands and in some cases millions of years at a rate averaging an inch (2.5 centimeters) per 500 years. The amount of soil available to farmers is now decreasing at an alarming rate, due mostly to wind and water erosion. In the US Great Plains, roughly half the quantity in place at the beginning of the last century is now gone. In Australia, after two centuries of European land-use, more than 70 percent of land has become seriously degraded. Erosion is largely a function of tillage, which fractures and loosens soil; thus, as the introduction of fuel-fed tractors has increased the ease of tillage, the rate of soil loss has increased dramatically.

Farmers as a Percentage of the Population

In the US at the turn of the last century, 70 percent of the population lived in rural areas and farmed. Today less than two percent of Americans farm for a living. This change came about primarily because fuel-fed farm machinery replaced labor, which meant that fewer farmers were needed. Another way of saying this is that economies of scale (driven by mechanization) gave an advantage to ever-larger farms. But the loss of farmers also meant a gradual loss of knowledge of how to farm and a loss of rural farming culture. Many farmers today merely follow the directions on bags of fertilizer or pesticide, and live so far from their neighbors that their children have no desire to continue the agricultural way of life.

On top of these long-term trends, four more recent related trends spell trouble for the continuance of current fuel-based agricultural production.

Grain Production per Capita

A total of 2,029 million tons (1,841 metric tons) of grain were produced globally in 2004; this was a record in absolute numbers. But for the past two decades population has grown faster than grain production, so there is actually less available on a per-head basis. In addition, grain stocks are being drawn down. According to Lester Brown of the Earth Policy Institute, "in each of the last four...years production fell short of consumption. The shortfalls of nearly 100 million tons in 2002 and again in 2003 were the largest on record."[15] This suggests that the strategy of boosting food production by the use of fossil fuels is already yielding diminishing returns.

Global Climate

This is being increasingly destabilized as a result of the global greenhouse effect, resulting in farming problems that are relatively minor now but that are likely to grow to catastrophic proportions within the next decade or two. Global warming is now almost universally acknowledged as resulting from CO_2 emissions from the burning of fossil fuels.

Available Fresh Water

In the US, 85 percent of fresh water use goes toward agricultural production, requiring the drawing down of ancient aquifers at far above their recharge rates. Globally, as water tables fall, ever more powerful pumps must be used to lift irrigation water, requiring ever more energy usage. By 2020, according to the WorldWatch Institute and the UN, virtually every country will face shortages of fresh water.

The Effectiveness of Pesticides and Herbicides
In the US, pesticide use increased 33-fold between 1945 and 1990, and has remained at roughly the same level since. Yet each year a greater amount of agricultural produce is lost to pests, which are evolving immunities faster than chemists can invent new poisons. Like falling grain production per capita, this trend suggests a declining return from injecting the process of agricultural production with still more fossil fuels.

Now, let us add to this picture the inevitable peak in world oil production, which will make machinery more expensive to operate, fertilizers and other agricultural chemicals more expensive to produce and purchase, and the transportation of both chemical inputs and agricultural products more costly. While the adoption of fossil fuels created a range of problems for global food production (as it also substantially increased the amount of food available), the decline in the availability of cheap oil will not immediately solve those problems; in fact, over the short term it will exacerbate them, bringing simmering crises to a boil.

That is because the scale of our dependency on fossil fuels has grown to such enormous proportions.

In the US, agriculture is directly responsible for well over 10 percent of all national energy consumption. Over 400 gallons (1,818 liters) of oil equivalent are expended to feed each American each year.[17] About a third of that amount (mostly in the form of natural gas) goes toward fertilizer production, 20 percent to operate machinery, 16 percent for transportation, 13 percent for irrigation, 8 percent for livestock raising (not including the feed), and 5 percent for pesticide production. This does not include energy costs for packaging, refrigeration, transportation to retailers, or cooking.[18]

Trucks move most of the world's food, even though trucking is many times more energy-intensive than moving food by train or ship. Refrigerated jets move a small but growing proportion of food, almost entirely to wealthy industrial nations, at up to 50 times the energy cost of sea transport.

Processed foods make up three-quarters of global food sales by price (though not by quantity). This adds dramatically to energy costs. For example, a one-pound (450 gram) box of breakfast cereal may require over 7,000 kilocalories of energy for processing, while the cereal itself provides only 1,100 kilocalories of food energy.[19]

Over all—including energy costs for farm machinery, transportation, and processing, and oil and natural gas used as feedstocks for agricultural chemicals—the modern food system consumes roughly ten calories of fossil-fuel energy for every calorie of food energy produced.[20]

But the single most telling gauge of our dependency is the size of the global population. Without fossil fuels powering agricultural machinery, producing fertilizer, pumping water, and transporting food, the stupendous growth in human numbers that has occurred over the past century would have been impossible. Perhaps the most important challenge we will face in the coming century will be that of continuing to support our existing and still growing population as the availability of cheap oil declines.

In the US, in the early winter of 2005–2006, during the run-up in gasoline, diesel, and natural gas prices following hurricanes Katrina and Rita, thousands of farmers across the nation agonized over whether they could afford to plant the next year's crop.[21] This may be only a small indication of what is in store.

Facing steep and unpredictable prices for fuels and fertilizer, more and more farmers will likely go bankrupt. Eventually, increasing food production costs must be passed on to consumers, and food will become more expensive relative to the buying power of citizens. This raises the specter of increasing levels of hunger and malnourishment, perhaps even in relatively wealthy nations.

War and Geopolitics

During the 20th Century as petroleum came to be seen as a strategic resource, competition for oil erupted into conflict on many occasions.

During the latter years of the 19th Century and the early decades of the 20th Century, Baku on the Caspian Sea was a main source of the world's oil exports. It became an international city, featuring grand villas built by locals and foreigners who benefited from the region's oil riches. During World War I Baku's oil was a target for the German army, and in 1918–1919 the British briefly occupied the region. Soon it was taken by the newly formed USSR, so that Caspian oil could fuel Soviet industrialization.

The Japanese attack on Pearl Harbor was triggered, at least in part, by the United States' decision to cut off oil exports to Japan in 1941, an action taken in response to Japanese pursuit of a Pacific empire. Japan, which had been almost completely reliant on imported oil, mainly from the US, concluded that it would have to obtain its oil elsewhere. This was a factor in its invasion of the oil-rich Dutch East Indies

Historians of the Second World War now generally agree that Adolf Hitler planned to capture the oilfields of Romania by 1939 so that Germany would have a supply of oil. The next stages of the strategy included capture the oilfields of Persia by 1941, and those of Russia in 1942. However, America entered the war before these goals could be accomplished, and the allies managed to deny Hitler access to precious petroleum.

For the past several decades the West has sought to secure the Middle East as a main source of fuels. Decades before oil was discovered there, Britain became involved diplomatically in the Arabian Gulf region as a result of maritime interests. Then, with the discovery of several important Gulf oilfields in the 1930s, the region's perceived strategic value increased significantly, and other powers—including Germany, Russia, and the United States—began to exercise influence there as well.

Oil played a part in a 1953 coup in Iran organized by the US and Britain against the elected prime minister, Mohammed Mossadegh, who had nationalized the assets of the British-owned Anglo Iranian oil company (the forerunner of British Petroleum, or BP).

The oil embargo of 1973 demonstrated the possibility of using the withholding of oil supplies as a form of economic weapon; during the embargo, the US was so concerned about restoring access to Arabian Gulf oil that it contemplated invading and occupying the Middle East, as has been revealed by documents recently released from the British National Archives.[22]

Military operations against Iraq undertaken by the United States and its allies as a result of Saddam Hussein's invasion of Kuwait in 1991 (which was itself motivated in no small part by conflicts over ownership of oilfields) were primarily driven by the need to maintain secure access to Middle Eastern oil—not just for the US, but for Europe and Japan as well—and to prevent Hussein from expanding his control over

oil flows from the region. Moreover, although the more recent American-British invasion of Iraq was ostensibly undertaken to find banned weapons, oil was unquestionably a
factor—as US Vice President Dick Cheney made clear in a
statement in August 2002, in which he warned that "Saddam
Hussein could then be expected to seek domination of the
entire Middle East [and] take control of a great proportion
of the world's energy supplies...."[23]

Competition for the wealth provided by oil has been a
source of civil conflict within nations, with historic or current instances occurring in Nigeria and Sudan. Petroleum
wealth has also fueled internal abuses of power. In this regard, Saddam Hussein offers the prime example: it was his
country's oil revenues that enabled him to assemble one of
the largest armies in the Gulf region.

In the future, as oil grows more scarce and valuable,
conflicts over oil are likely to become more frequent and
deadly, both within and between nations. Currently, militarily powerful oil-importing nations maintain bases in many
oil-producing regions, and in sensitive or disputed transship-
ment or pipeline areas. United Press International recently
quoted a top US energy official as saying that "more than half
of the US defense budget goes to protecting energy coming
from unstable areas of the world."[24] Possible future sites of
conflict include most of the places where sizable exploitable
oil deposits remain: the South China Sea, West Africa, South
America, the Middle East, and Central Asia.

Competition between major oil importers is almost certain to escalate as global production rates falter. One study
paper by an American military analyst (Major Chris Jeffries,
Assistant Professor at the US Air Force Academy) even suggests that the United States and Europe might eventually

come into open conflict over dwindling Middle East oil supplies.[25]

Other scenarios are easier to imagine—such as ones in which a major oil-exporting nation decides to withhold its resources from the world market in order to drive up prices or to obtain a political advantage; or in which a major producer, or group of producers, decides to embargo a major importer, or to favor one importer over another, for political reasons.

It hardly needs to be stressed that modern weaponry could make future oil wars extremely destructive and lethal. Ironically, a large-scale open conflict would almost certainly use and destroy large quantities of the very substance being fought over. (During the Iraq war of 1991, roughly 11 million barrels of oil were drained into the Arabian Gulf while up to 190 oil wells in Kuwait were set ablaze, with nearly a billion barrels of crude consumed by fire.) In the end, no one could be said to win such a war.

Terrorism

The term *terrorism* is generally understood to mean political violence that is part of a strategy of coordinated attacks falling outside the bounds of conventional warfare. While this kind of violence has a long history, widespread concern about it has mounted over the past few decades as a result of several spectacular and deadly incidents, notably those in New York and Washington on September 11, 2001.

There is considerable controversy regarding the causes of terrorism. Academic inquiries have centered on four classes of explanation:

• *Sociological explanations,* which focus on the position of the perpetrators in society (e.g., poverty and powerlessness).

- *Conflict theory,* which examines their relationship to those in power (e.g., lack of legitimate outlets for dissent).
- *Ideological explanations,* which focus on the differences in religion or political ideology.
- *Media theory explanations,* which treat terrorist acts as a means of communication.

Poor governance by regimes that provide few legitimate political opportunities for opposition appears in many cases to be a significant contributing factor. Further, a combination of poor governance and weak economic management may result in under-employment among people who are young and relatively well-educated, whose political frustrations are then exploited by religious extremist groups. Also, nations with weak governments can provide attractive havens for terrorists.[26]

However, these general explanations must be seen in context. The instances of terrorism that especially concern Western nations today seem to be associated with countries which happen to be important producers and exporters of oil. It would be shortsighted not to view such instances of terrorism in light of the long history of interference by the West in the politics of these nations. Given the deep-seated sense of grievance felt by many people in these relatively poor, resource-exporting countries on one hand, and the growing dependence and therefore vulnerability among people in relatively wealthy industrialized (and in some cases militarily powerful) resource-importing nations on the other, the eruption of asymmetrical and unconventional forms of conflict between the two should perhaps come as no surprise.

It is certainly not our intent here to condone terrorist

methods; rather, it is merely to show how the motivation for some terrorist incidents may be related to historic, current, and future aspects of the global oil trade, and to suggest how the motivation for at least some future terrorist acts may be removed or reduced by systematically altering the nature of that trade.

Let us consider the published statements of Osama bin Laden as an expression of the sentiment motivating the sorts of terrorist incidents we are discussing. Bin Laden has consistently decried the presence of American troops in Saudi Arabia as well as Israel's occupation of Palestine and control of the city of Jerusalem. Bin Laden told ABC News in 1998, "In today's wars there are no morals. [Western nations] *rip us of our wealth and of our resources and of our oil* [emphasis added]. Our religion is under attack. They kill and murder our brothers. They compromise our honor and our dignity...." More recently he has said that "One of the most important reasons that made our enemies control our land is the pilfering of our oil...."[27]

Moreover, if bin Laden and Al Qaeda see oil as a source of the resentment they evidently hold toward the West, they also view the West's dependence on Middle Eastern oil as a vulnerability they can exploit. Bin Laden says, for example, "Be active and prevent them from reaching the oil, and mount your operations accordingly, particularly in Iraq and the Gulf, for this is their fate."[28] According to Middle Eastern analyst Christopher M. Blanchard, writing for the US Congressional Research Service:

> Bin Laden's statements reveal sophisticated consideration of the economic and military vulnerabilities of the United States and its allies, particularly with regard to the role of

Middle Eastern oil as "the basis of industry" in the global economy. Bin Laden has called for Muslim societies to become more self-sufficient economically and has urged Arab governments to preserve oil as "a great and important economic power for the coming Islamic state." Bin Laden also has described economic boycotts as "extremely effective" weapons. Bin Laden's recent descriptions of Al Qaeda's "bleed-until-bankruptcy plan" and his discussion of the U.S. economy and the decreasing value of the U.S. dollar fit his established pattern of citing the economic effects of terrorist attacks as proof of Al Qaeda's success. Recent statements urging attacks on oil pipelines and military supply lines could indicate a shift in Al Qaeda's strategic and tactical planning in favor of a more protracted attritional conflict characterized by disruptive attacks on economic and critical infrastructure.[29]

According to the International Energy Agency, the proportion of the global oil supply coming from OPEC nations can only increase in the years ahead. As the price of oil escalates and as increasing amounts of wealth are therefore transferred to oil exporters from oil importers, the latter may be ever more highly motivated to try to control political and economic affairs in oil-rich regions. For people living in these regions (which happen to be ones in which high national oil revenues are typically not reflected in per-capita incomes), such external efforts to exert control may be seen as further cause for resentment and therefore for terrorist actions. But if competition for oil fuels further terrorism, increasing instances of terrorism will in turn trigger more oil price volatility (already many analysts believe that the world price of petroleum includes a "terrorism premium" of $10 or more per barrel), and therefore more competition for the resource wherever it exists, setting up a self-reinforcing feed-back loop. Thus even if terrorism does not have its ultimate origin in resource disputes, its proximate causes will likely proliferate and deepen given current trends having to do with our society's petroleum dependency and oil's increasing scarcity.

With the Protocol

Taken together, these extrapolated trends and potentials are nothing less than horrifying. As global oil production enters its inevitable decline, we must contemplate the likelihood that the remainder of the current century will be filled with dramatically heightened risks of resource wars, terrorism, economic collapse, and widespread hunger.

We must stress once again that our assessment is not exaggerated. Every forecast or scenario described above is drawn from the work of competent, independent analysts inside and outside government, from various nations, and from a range of political backgrounds.

Even though the future without an Oil Depletion Protocol is likely to be perilous, there is no guarantee that acceptance of the Protocol will avert all of the dangers described above. Nevertheless, many of the worst of them may be avoided or ameliorated significantly. Clearly, a cooperative effort by the world's nations will accomplish more toward easing the inevitably painful transition away from petroleum than will ruthless competition for what remains of a resource that is becoming ever scarcer.

The Global Economy

If substitutes for oil cannot be developed quickly enough (and this is a strong likelihood, as documented in the Hirsch Report), the only way to maintain price stability in a post-

Peak world will be some method of global rationing, of which the Oil Depletion Protocol would be the simplest and most straightforward. If the Protocol were generally adopted, oil prices would likely relatively remain high by historic standards, but would also be comparatively stable and predictable. This would facilitate long-range planning, which will be essential to the economic survival of entire industries and companies of all sizes, as well as cities and nations. Knowing how much fuel they will have available, and at approximately what price, nations would be able to forge strategies for a gradual transition to a petroleum-free future.

Transportation

The effects of the Protocol for the transportation sector follow from those noted immediately above: stable prices and an assurance of predictably declining future supply would enable individuals to plan their modes of travel, and would create strong incentives for cities and nations to begin a transition to the production of more efficient vehicles and a switch to less energy-intensive transportation systems. Industries and companies that rely upon transport of raw materials and manufactured goods, and transport companies, would also be able to plan more effectively. National governments would be motivated to assist with the transition by subsidizing more efficient transport modes.

Food and Agriculture

With stable prices of predictably diminishing oil, countries would be faced with the difficult but manageable challenge of converting their food production to a non-petroleum regime. This would mean gradually reducing fossil-fuel inputs and also minimizing the transport of food. These are tasks that will require many years of sustained effort, which would be made enormously easier if fuel prices could be controlled in the meantime.

War and Geopolitics

General adoption of the Oil Depletion Protocol would entail nations agreeing to produce, sell, and use less oil on a yearly basis, with all amounts monitored and reported transparently. This would remove incentives to engage in geopolitical maneuvering for advantage in either the export or the import sphere. Diminished competition would mean a substantially reduced likelihood of conflict—between importing nations, between importers and exporters, and within oil-rich nations over internal control of resource wealth.

Terrorism

The general adoption of the Oil Depletion Protocol would probably not bring an immediate end to terrorism. Some terrorism that is not related even indirectly to oil will not be affected at all. However, with a reduction in the need for petroleum-importing nations to control political events in exporting nations, there is likely to be a gradual lessening of some important historic causes of the most spectacular and worrisome recent instances of terrorism. Clearly, reducing terrorism by eliminating its causes would be far cheaper and more effective in every respect than trying to do away with it by killing or imprisoning all of the people who are or might be drawn to join or support terrorist groups.

In sum, without the Oil Depletion Protocol the possible consequences of Peak Oil for every sector of every society are likely to be profound and overwhelmingly damaging. While the Protocol cannot insulate individuals, companies, industries, countries, or the world as a whole from all of those potential impacts, it has the potential to reduce risks to such a degree as to more than justify the considerable efforts that will be required to overcome the political and social resistance to its adoption.

3

A Plan

WHEN A RESOURCE becomes scarce, modern societies typically address the problem in one of three ways. All are, strictly speaking, forms of *rationing*—which is the controlled distribution of resources and goods.

First, resources and products can be rationed by price. In this case, the market handles distribution. Those who are able to pay and who want a resource or product the most can obtain the largest quantity. In the case of luxury goods, or in instances where shortfalls are minor and temporary, this presents no problem. However, in the case of serious, lingering shortages of necessary resources and goods (water, food, housing, and energy), rationing by price can result in a situation where a resource becomes so expensive that many cannot afford enough even to meet basic needs, while others with plenty of money experience no hardship and consume much more than they actually require. In some instances, this in turn can create the conditions for civil or international conflict. Historically, even in free-market economies, price rationing has sometimes been rejected in wartime (when domestic unity is at a premium) and in cases of food or energy scarcity.

Price controls represent another way of dealing with scarcity. In this case, effort is directed toward combating the negative consequences of price rationing by simply preventing sellers from raising prices. Price controls are intuitively appealing to consumers for obvious reasons. However, such controls do not increase the quantity of resources or goods available, and do not reduce demand (which high prices effectively do, up to a point); in fact, artificially low prices actually encourage demand, which cannot be satisfied by the available supply—a situation that creates long queues and general frustration.[1] Experience shows that price ceilings discourage producers from investing more in production, a situation that can actually exacerbate shortages. Thus economists generally oppose this strategy, except in very brief emergency situations. An especially relevant example occurred during the oil crisis of 1973, when the US government instituted controls capping the price of "old oil" (already discovered) while allowing the price of newly discovered oil to float; this resulted in a withdrawal of old oil from the market. The rule, which was intended to spur more exploration, simply exacerbated the existing oil scarcity.[2]

Finally there is rationing by quota. In Britain during World War I, panic buying prompted quota rationing first of sugar, then meat. During World War II, quota rationing was practiced in many countries, including the United States. Governments issued books of ration coupons to citizens, who could present the coupons at stores. Items still had to be paid for. Many people were actually better nourished under food rationing programs than previously: infant mortality due to poor nutrition declined in both Britain and the US during World War II. More recently, in the summer of 2001 when low water levels threatened Brazil's hydro-dependent electricity grid system, that nation instituted electricity rationing, with cuts of 20 percent mandated for domestic users and businesses and stiff penalties for non-compliance. The rules were eased in November with the arrival of the rainy season.[3]

With quota rationing, the government must undertake the difficult job of adjusting quotas to reflect fluctuating supplies and the needs of individual consumers. While an equal quota for each consumer makes sense in a few cases—bread in a city under siege is the classic example—most rationing programs must face the problem that consumer needs vary widely. In the case of fuel, some motorists need to drive more because they commute long distances and thus require more gasoline, while others need drive very little.

In this book we are considering the impending global consequences of our use of oil—a depleting, non-renewable resource. A substantial reduction in usage will require coordinated effort. Because we will in effect be collectively managing whatever petroleum resources remain, the strategy we adopt will constitute a form of rationing. We have already (in Chapter 2) argued that, as petroleum becomes scarce, price rationing will lead to a range of catastrophic consequences. Price controls have historically been ineffective and even counterproductive, and so we need not waste much time exploring that option. Nor is quota rationing imaginable on a global scale although, as we will discuss in Chapter 5, it could work well at the national level.

Clearly, there must be other ways of approaching the problem, but the following questions quickly arise: How would a global rationing scheme work? How would it be enforced? Should it concern just oil, or all fossil fuels? Should it treat all nations similarly, or should it favor nations that have previously had less opportunity to enjoy oil-fuelled industrialization? Let us sort through the options.

Emissions-Based Proposals

In the mid-1990s, widespread concern about the looming climatic consequences of emissions from the burning of fossil fuels led to the negotiation of the Kyoto Protocol, which mandates a reduction in the emission of greenhouse gases (principally carbon dioxide) to levels 5.2 percent below those in 1990; this is to be achieved by industrial countries by the year 2012. Non-industrial nations are exempted for the time being, though negotiations are intended to begin soon on cuts to be made by the developing world.

The Kyoto Protocol does not represent an instance of rationing in the usual sense, since the objective is not to distribute a scarce resource but to reduce the negative environmental consequences of the use of a certain kind of resource. Nevertheless, it can be seen as a form of rationing in the broadest sense of the term, as it works by first creating emissions rights and then controlling their distribution.

While nearly the whole world has embraced the Kyoto Protocol, the US—which emits more greenhouse gases than any other country—has refused to ratify it, as has Australia. For the past several years, this led many analysts to conclude that the Protocol was, in effect, dead. However, in December, 2005 at the Conference on Climate in Montreal, negotiators from over 180 nations agreed to begin work on tougher emissions targets to come into force after 2012; the US, isolated in its opposition, agreed at the last moment to join industrializing nations like China in an "open and non-binding" dialogue about how to make their own contributions to reducing carbon emissions.

Negotiators of Kyoto (and whatever follows) have three conflicting constituencies to satisfy:

- Those who complain that implementation will curtail economic growth.
- Those who say that the mandated emissions reductions are insufficient (climate scientists say that cuts of up to 80 percent by mid-century will be needed in order to avert catastrophic climate change).
- Those who say that as long as the more industrialized nations continue to use fossil fuels at a higher rate than the rest of the world, less-industrialized nations should not be required to reduce their emissions at all.

According to a press release from the United Nations Environment Programme:

> The Kyoto Protocol is an agreement under which industrialized countries will reduce their collective emissions of greenhouse gases by 5.2% compared to the year 1990 (but note that, compared to the emissions levels that would be expected by 2010 without the Protocol, this target represents a 29% cut). The goal is to lower overall emissions from six greenhouse gases—carbon dioxide, methane, nitrous oxide, sulfur hexafluoride, HFCs, and PFCs—calculated as an average over the five-year period of 2008–12. National targets range from 8% reductions for the European Union and some others to 7% for the US, 6% for Japan, 0% for Russia, and permitted increases of 8% for Australia and 10% for Iceland.[4]

Each country agrees to limit emissions to the levels described in the Kyoto Protocol, but in the case of many countries those limits are above their current production. These "extra amounts" can be traded or sold to other nations on the open market. Russia, for example, which can easily meet its targets, can sell its carbon credits for millions of dollars to countries that will have more difficulty meeting their targets—such as Canada. This provides a financial incentive for nations to meet their targets as soon as possible. Countries also receive credits for various shared "clean energy" programs, as well as for providing "carbon dioxide sinks" in the form of forests or other systems that remove CO_2 from the atmosphere.

Some organizations believe that the Kyoto Protocol, while a step in the right direction, could be improved upon. Perhaps the most widely discussed alternative proposal is Contraction and Convergence (C&C), which is promoted by the Global Commons Institute.[5] C&C envisions "CO_2 Emissions Entitlements" consistent with an outcome of CO_2 concentrations in the atmosphere of 450 parts per million (ppm) by the year 2100 (the CO_2 level was just 278 ppm in pre-industrial times, while the current concentration is about 380 ppm). Where C&C especially differs from Kyoto is in the allotment of emissions entitlements not to nations, but to individuals worldwide on an equal per-capita basis (though this is not an immediate requirement but rather a target to be achieved by mid-century—hence the term "convergence"). The reasoning is simple: the Earth's atmosphere is a "global commons" of which each human being, regardless of nationality, has an equal share in terms of rights to pollute.[6]

The Global Commons Institute thus sees its plan as a way of solving two problems at once—global climate change and global economic inequity.

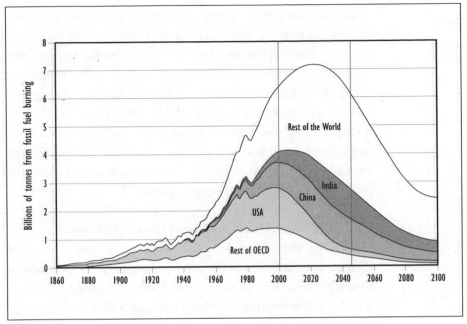

FIGURE 3.1. Comprehensive (all-country) Contraction and Convergence Scenario.
(CREDIT: Global Commons Institute.)

Figure 3.1 shows a CO_2 scenario under Contraction and
Convergence.

The Foundation for the Economics of Sustainability
(FEASTA), based in Ireland, supports Contraction and Convergence goals including the strategy of issuing equal per-
capita tradable emissions rights. However, FEASTA argues
that this system of allocation, while equitable, would still not
be sufficiently fair, as people living in some parts of the world
have challenges to overcome before they can live as comfort-
ably on their emissions allocation as people elsewhere. In a
departure from the Global Commons Institute's version of
C&C, therefore, FEASTA proposes that, for the first two
decades after C&C commences, everyone should receive the

same allocation each year but at the rate appropriate for year
20. The difference between the total amount of emissions
permits available for any particular year and the amount distributed to individuals (represented by the shaded area above
the dotted line in Figure 3.2) would go into a "convergence
fund" to be allocated to national governments according to
an internationally-agreed, transparent set of criteria. National governments could sell their emissions permits to raise
funds for projects that enabled their countries to make the
transition to lower fossil energy use.

How Fossil Fuel Emissions Rights Could be Shared

Under the plan proposed by FEASTA, the world's carbon
dioxide emissions would be cut back annually, as represented
by the sloping line. Each year, the entire emissions allocation
would be shared equally among the world population except
during the first, say, twenty years, when some of the allocation (represented by the hatched area) would be issued to
governments to enable them to make their economies less reliant on fossil fuels.

In 2005 the EU initiated an emissions trading system in
which ration coupons were given to big emitters, allowing
them to increase their profits by selling the coupons which
they received at no cost. FEASTA has critiqued this system,
suggesting that the EU system be reformed from 2008 on-
ward so that the permits are given to the people, not the
companies—which would buy them through the banking
system from the people. This could be the forerunner for a
global system along the same lines.

FEASTA also supports the creation of an emissions-based
global currency unit (the Ebcu), whose use would at once

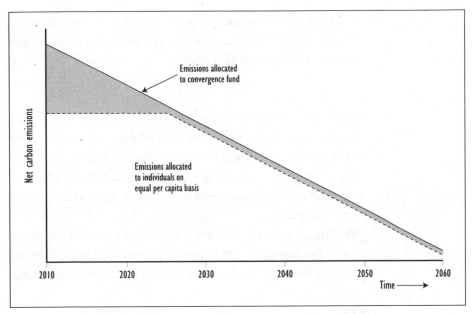

FIGURE 3.2.   FEASTA emissions reduction scenario. (CREDIT: FEASTA.)

stabilize the global economy, wipe out poorer nations' debts, and encourage a transition to renewable energy sources. Here is FEASTA's summary of its proposals regarding currency reform:

Global
- A genuine world currency should be established.
- This new world currency should be issued by being given into circulation rather than lent.
- The initial distribution of the new currency should be on the basis of population rather than economic power.
- Over the years, the supply of the new currency should be limited in a way that ensures that the overall volume of

world trade is compatible with whatever is considered to be the most crucial area of global sustainability. In our view, this is the world climate.

National
- Each country or monetary union should operate two currencies, one for normal commercial exchanges, the other for savings and capital transfers. Each of these currencies would have its own floating exchange rate with the new international currency, and hence a variable exchange rate with the other.
- The new national exchange currencies would be spent into circulation by their governments rather than being created through the banking system on the basis of debt.

Local
- The establishment of regional (i.e. sub-national) and local exchange currencies should be encouraged.[6]

Finally, FEASTA also advocates the creation of a fossil fuel buyers' organization that would negotiate with oil and gas producing countries for supplies. The organization and the producers would agree on a fixed price for whatever amounts of coal, oil, and gas could be produced and exported each year. The buyers' organization would set up a system to share out the amount of the fuels purchased among the participating countries using the Contraction and Convergence allocation method.

A Depletion-Based Proposal
In our view, any proposal that reduces fossil fuel dependency and greenhouse gas emissions is a step in the right direction. Thus in proposing an Oil Depletion Protocol we are not ar-

guing against any of these emissions-based proposals; we are instead offering another option—one that begins from a different premise, that may offer some distinct advantages, and that could be implemented in concert with emissions-based agreements.

Most emissions-based proposals (except FEASTA's) assume that enough fossil-fuel resources exist to continue fuelling industrial societies far into the future at current rates of demand growth. The problem, again in the view of the proponents of such proposals, is that continued use of fossil fuels yields emissions (CO_2) that are destabilizing the Earth's climate, a process likely to lead in turn to ecological and economic catastrophe within the current century. Thus the strategy adopted is voluntary curtailment to avoid environmental harm. However, some plans also seek to apportion this curtailment in such a way as to foster global economic equity.

The present depletion-based proposal starts with the recognition that the most important fossil fuel from an economic perspective (petroleum) is going to become scarce and expensive within the near future. Thus the nations of the world *will* reduce usage of at least some fossil fuels whether they do so deliberately or not, because available supply will not be sufficient to feed the demand that would exist were prices to remain at historic levels. Indeed, the available supply in terms of deliverable flow rates will begin to shrink, and the scale of the cumulative decrease over the course of, say, two decades following the peak is likely to be substantial. This in itself presents the world with an enormous problem, one that will likely lead to serious economic and geopolitical dilemmas. The challenge in this case, then, will be to reduce petroleum dependency in national economies cooperatively and systematically so as to avert economic collapse, civil unrest, terrorism, and war.

The climate-change movement has been advocating for many years a reduction in fossil fuel usage. Peak Oil means categorically that such a reduction is not optional—it will be forced upon us by nature at some point. If we do not plan for that event and reduce our dependency now, the consequences then will likely be dire. While it is true that we will be able to replace petroleum to some extent with fuels synthesized from other fossil sources (using coal-to-liquids and gas-to-liquids technologies, as well as extra-heavy oil and oil shale), and perhaps as well with biofuels, it will probably not be possible to increase the extraction, conversion, or production of these materials fast enough to make up for likely declines in global oil production rates. Thus in dealing with Peak Oil the nations of the world will have to rely primarily on strategies that emphasize demand reduction. The implementation of such strategies is likely to result also in a substantial reduction of greenhouse gas emissions.

Further, while emissions-based proposals focus on the economic benefit of burning fossil fuels and thus seek equity by demanding the largest reductions from those using the most, an Oil Depletion Protocol is likely to highlight instead the economic vulnerability created by oil dependence, and mandate equal cuts in production and imports for all countries that participate, recognizing that countries that make the transition away from petroleum sooner will be at a great economic advantage over those that put off the effort until later. This being the case, requiring a slower transition by poorer nations would actually offer them no advantage in the long run: whatever infrastructure they were to build using additional fossil fuels would likely only create more fossil-fuel dependency that would have to be dealt with later, when the means for doing so might not be as readily available.

Throughout the remainder of this book we will devote

most of our attention to the possible terms and outcomes of an Oil Depletion Protocol, rather than emissions-based proposals, because information on the latter is available elsewhere. At the end of this chapter we will briefly discuss how emissions-based and depletion-based proposals might complement one another in practice.

Basic vs. Ancillary Provisions

The title of this book might give the impression that there is only a single Oil Depletion Protocol, and this is true in the sense that so far only one has been seriously proposed—that outlined by Dr. Colin J. Campbell, founder of the Association for the Study of Peak Oil.[7] However, just as there are several suggestions for emissions-based agreements, there could be other approaches to a depletion-based accord.[8] Any Oil Depletion Protocol must consist essentially of a cooperative plan to reduce petroleum imports and production. Ways of reducing dependency might include taxes and fees on petroleum consumption, or subsidies and other incentives to encourage investment in other energy sources. The transformation of urban infrastructure to reduce the need for transportation and to support mass transit systems might also be encouraged using fees and incentives. In addition, it is possible to imagine complex subsidiary agreements to reform currencies, forgive past debts, or foster global economic equity. Once again, however, the core of the agreement must be clearly and simply to reduce world oil dependency.

How much and how fast? One can envision a range of formulas for the percentage of reduction in oil usage (production and exports). Clearly, the best formula would be one that is not seen as arbitrary (otherwise negotiations could be endless), and one that is easy to understand.

Colin Campbell, in his proposed Protocol, has suggested

a formula based on depletion rates that would work as follows: importers would reduce their imports by the world oil
depletion rate, while producing countries would reduce
their rate of production by their national depletion rate.

The concept of the depletion rate is simple to grasp given
a little thought. Clearly, each country has a finite endowment
of oil from nature; thus, when the first barrel has been extracted, there is accordingly one less left for the future. What
is left for the future consists of two elements: first, how much
remains in known oilfields (termed remaining reserves) and
second, how much remains to be found in the future (termed
yet-to-find). How much is yet-to-find may be reasonably estimated by extrapolating the discovery trend of the past. The
depletion rate equals the total yet-to-produce divided by the
yearly amount currently being extracted.

Let us take a hypothetical producing country with 1000
million barrels of oil yet-to-produce and that is extracting 30
million barrels per year. This yields a depletion rate of 3
percent. By the second year of the agreement, that nation's
amount yet-to-produce will have declined by 30 million
barrels to 970 Mb. Our hypothetical nation could produce 3
percent of that amount, or 29.1 million barrels, or exactly 3
percent less than the previous year. (New discoveries or reserve upgradings would not affect the situation appreciably,
as future discovery estimates are incorporated into the depletion rate from the beginning).

Thus the depletion rate is also the amount by which production would be *reduced* each year. For importing countries, this would be similarly true with regard to the world
depletion rate (currently calculated by Dr. Campbell at 2.6
percent per annum). This would be the percentage by which
importers would reduce their imports each year.

Again, other formulas for reducing world oil dependency are imaginable; however, because Campbell's formula is non-arbitrary, intuitively graspable by the layperson, and within the range of percentages that would likely be negotiable in any case, we shall use it as the basis for the remainder of our discussion regarding the likely content of an Oil Depletion Protocol.

Advantages

Reducing production and imports in this fashion would yield a number of advantages, not all of them immediately obvious.

First, it would conserve the resource. Petroleum engineers are keenly aware that oilfields that are depleted too quickly can be damaged, resulting in a reduction in the total amount eventually recoverable. Voluntarily and systematically reducing the rate at which the world's oilfields are depleted would extend their lifetimes, so that future generations could have access to a resource of which there is a finite quantity and that is useful for a wide range of purposes—both as a machine lubricant, and as a feedstock for the production of pharmaceuticals, chemicals, and plastics—other than simply as a fuel.

Second, from the standpoint of reducing carbon emissions, the cumulative reduction in oil consumption globally would be substantial—in ten years, a total of about 35 percent reduction.

Third, from the standpoint of the participating nations, the reductions would be gradual and foreseeable. Nations, municipalities, and businesses would be able to plan their economic futures with minimal concern for dramatic price variations for oil and oil products, since there would likely be more world spare petroleum production capacity than would be the case without a Protocol, and thus a greater ability to adjust to short-term causes of shortages—including geopolitical conflict, accident, and natural disaster.

The Secretariat; Enforcement

Who would keep track of proven reserves, production, imports and exports, and who would estimate each country's oil yet-to-be-found, and prevent cheating? Clearly, if a Depletion Protocol were to be enacted, an international agency would have to be empowered to do these things. But this raises further questions: How big an organization would be required? Who would set it up? How would it be financed? What powers of enforcement would it have? And how would it avoid outside political influence?

These are difficult questions to answer, but they are the kinds of questions that must be dealt with in the creation of any international accord. For example, The Montreal Protocol on ozone-depleting chemicals (1987) and the Convention on Long-Range Transboundary Air Pollution (LRTAP, 1979) are notable for having developed institutional structures that have not only implemented their original agreements, but allowed additions to and refinements of those agreements. In the case of LRTAP, this structure includes an Executive Body, which meets annually; a Working Group on Strategies, which is a unique mixture of scientists and policy makers; a monitoring program (EMEP); and a secretariat. This structure has facilitated the adoption of five protocols to the Convention, with further protocols in the pipeline.

Clearly, the preference would be for the smallest structure possible that has the power to do the things required of it. In view of the importance of the Protocol and the benefits accruing from it, the financing of a secretariat and a monitoring agency should not pose a problem: member nations could pay for both according to a simple formula based on the scale of their consumption. The secretariat would have to be empowered by member nations to assess and enforce financial penalties for countries that refuse data or cheat.

Calculating Depletion Rates

The following are some provisions that the Protocol, even in its most parsimonious form, would likely contain.

The first job of the secretariat would be to undertake a systematic audit of global oil reserves to enable the calculation of the world depletion rate. It is important that this be done using a transparent and consistent methodology.

The secretariat would publish statistics annually, updating the world depletion rate as new data became available.

Member nations would have to agree to complete transparency regarding reserves, discovery, and production. They would be required to submit to an initial audit upon signing. This would facilitate not only the calculation of the world depletion rate, but also the national depletion rate for each producing country.

While national depletion rates would initially be calculated to take into account likely future discovery (based on extrapolation of past discovery trends), any producing nation could at any time request at its own expense a new audit and a recalculation of its depletion rate based upon new discoveries.

How to Define "Oil"?

Not all oil is the same. As well as conventional oil, there are several categories of non-conventional petroleum resources capable of being turned into synthetic liquid hydrocarbon fuels—including deepwater oil, heavy and extra-heavy oil (including oil sands), oil shale, polar oil, natural gas liquids and condensates, as well as coal and natural gas processed by means of coal-to-liquids and gas-to-liquids technologies.

These non-conventional resources may have characteristics quite different from those of conventional oil. For example, oil shale exists in vast deposits in western North America, as well as in Australia, Brazil, China, Estonia, France, Russia, Scotland, South Africa, Spain, and Sweden. However, the name "oil shale" is a misnomer, in that the organic material present is not oil *per se*, but kerogen, and the "shale" is usually a relatively hard rock called marl. Oil shale is burned directly as a very low-grade, high ash-content fuel in a few countries such as Estonia. Properly processed with heat, kerogen can be converted into a petroleum-like substance. While most historic efforts to do this on a commercial scale have failed, Shell has recently announced a successful experimental program to produce synthetic oil from marlstone by cooking the rock in place with underground heaters.[9] If Shell's process can be scaled up, then with favorable conditions oil shale may begin to make a modest contribution to the world's energy supply.

Clearly, however, including global shale oil deposits in a Depletion Protocol in the same category as conventional oil would dramatically and unrealistically skew depletion rates, reducing the world depletion rate from 2.6 percent to some small fraction of one percent. Similarly, treating the production from coal-to-liquids facilities like conventional oil would require including some substantial portion of global coal reserves as potential petroleum reserves, again skewing depletion rates downward.

The arguments for excluding deepwater and polar oil from treatment in an Oil Depletion Protocol are not as strong, as these resources are basically the same as conventional oil, but exist in environments where they are more difficult, expensive, or environmentally hazardous to access.

Nevertheless, the simplest and best course of action would likely be to define "oil" or "petroleum," for the purposes of the Protocol, as meaning only regular, conventional oil.

It might be objected that excluding non-conventional petroleum sources such as oil sands from the Depletion Protocol would privilege them, leading to a dramatic increase of production of liquid fuels from coal, natural gas, oil sands, and shale oil, defeating the purpose of the Protocol and resulting in increased carbon emissions into the atmosphere.

However, with the Depletion Protocol in place, prices of regular conventional oil will be kept stable and lower than they would otherwise be, so that demand for non-conventional hydrocarbon liquid fuels (which typically cost much more to produce and whose production rates are in most cases constrained by physical factors such as availability of fresh water) will be moderated. In any case, the other main check on non-conventional production must be robust global agreements to reduce hydrocarbon emissions into the atmosphere.

Technical Explanation: Examples of How the Protocol Would Work

It may be helpful to examine some real-world examples in order to see better how the Depletion Protocol would work.

Norway is a country that reports exceptionally accurate reserves estimates. The total produced to-date is 18.5 billion barrels (Gb), and 11.3 Gb remain in known fields, with about 2 left to find, giving a rounded total of 32 Gb. It follows that 13.5 Gb are left to produce. In 2004, 1.07 Gb were extracted, giving a depletion rate of 7.4 percent (1.07/13.5). This is a comparatively high rate, typical of an offshore environment.

In the case of the US (considering only the lower 48 states and excluding deepwater), the corresponding numbers are: produced to-date, 173 Gb; remaining reserves, 24 Gb; yet-to-find, 2 Gb—meaning that there are 26 Gb left. Annual production in 2004 was 1.3 Gb, giving a depletion rate of 5 percent (1.3/26).

For the world as a whole, 975 Gb have been produced; 772 remain in known fields; and an estimated 134 Gb are Yet-to-Find, meaning that 906 Gb are left. Production of conventional oil in 2004 was 24 Gb, so the depletion rate is 2.59 percent (24/906).

It must be stressed that current reserves estimates in the public domain are grossly unreliable, and one of the purposes of the Protocol is to secure better information. The assessed depletion rate for each country, and eventually for the world as whole, is subject to revision when better information becomes available, but the resulting correction of the depletion rate will not be large, probably causing it to vary by less than one percentage point.

The Depletion Protocol would require importers to reduce their imports by the world depletion rate (i.e., 2.6 percent) each year in order to put demand into balance with world supply. As stated earlier, producers would reduce their production according to their national depletion rate. Thus Norway would be required to reduce its production by 7.4 percent each year. However, that country's production is already declining at an even higher rate, and so the producer's restrictions in the Depletion Protocol would impose no burden on that country whatever.

This is far from being a unique situation: the imposition on most producing countries would be minor, since few can now increase their rate of production in any case and many are experiencing declining production for purely geological reasons, as is the case with Norway, the US, and over two dozen others.

Agreeing to produce less oil would not inhibit exploration because new finds would lower the national depletion rate, and thus permit a higher rate of export than would otherwise be the case.

The main thrust of the Protocol would be to require importers to cut imports, but the inclusion of producers in the provisions would stimulate greater cooperation between the two parties. Any indigenous production in a country that was a net importer would not be likely to provide that country with an unfair advantage, as production within most importing countries is already declining at a rate higher than the world depletion rate.

How users (both producers and non-producers) would deal internally with having less oil would be up to them. Since this is a vital and relevant subject, we will offer some suggestions in the next chapter.

How Emissions-Based and Depletion-Based Agreements Could Work Together

The Oil Depletion Protocol will be far more effective in achieving its goals if it works in tandem with a strong emissions-based accord—one, that is, that includes all nations and requires emissions reductions from all participants. Without such an agreement, many nations would be tempted to replace their reliance on oil with an increased use of coal. This would be especially likely in many poorer nations that currently burn oil to produce much of their electricity. However there is the possibility that even wealthy nations would turn to coal-to-liquids technologies to replace conventional transportation fuels. While clean coal technologies are being developed (using carbon sequestration methods), concern for the added financial costs might lead some nations to forego them. The transition away from petroleum is essential, but it must not be undertaken in a way that would result in climate chaos.

Just as a strong Kyoto accord is necessary to guide nations in implementing the Oil Depletion Protocol, the former would benefit from the addition of the latter. That is because the Oil Depletion Protocol acknowledges another powerful motive for the energy transition in addition to the threat of climate change—the non-negotiable fact of depletion, and the peaking and decline of world petroleum extraction. The world's climate experts tell us that we should reduce fossil fuel usage in order to avert future environmental catastrophe. Experts in oil depletion inform us that this reduction is not a matter of choice: it will occur sooner or later for purely geological reasons, and weaning ourselves from oil dependence voluntarily, cooperatively, and gradually now will be much less costly and disruptive than waiting until shortages arise.

The Depletion Protocol would make the implementation of the Kyoto accord much easier than would otherwise be the case. If the world becomes mired in economic disaster and resource wars following the global oil production peak, the emissions reduction programs mandated by Kyoto will be undermined: nations will seek every possible means of maintaining economic growth, and will likely turn back to fossil fuels for that purpose; in addition, nations' intense competition for remaining supplies will weaken the spirit of international cooperation required for the Kyoto Protocol to function. An Oil Depletion Protocol could provide a platform of economic and geopolitical stability on which nations could carry out the difficult work of emissions reduction, energy transition, currency reform, and debt relief.

Kyoto as currently structured is less than optimal because it excludes the nations with the fastest-growing emissions rates: the industrializing nations of Asia. These less-industrialized countries have not agreed to emissions reductions because they don't want to forego fuel-fed development and because they demand fairness in the face of decades of preferential use of fossil fuels by industrialized countries. Meanwhile the world's current biggest emissions producer won't sign on for fear that the agreement will reduce its economic growth and its competitiveness with fast-developing countries. The Oil Depletion Protocol cuts through both objections by offering a simple formula for all countries to follow.

The Oil Depletion Protocol can be criticized because, in itself, it does nothing to address the problem of inequity (which C&C does explicitly, and Kyoto to a lesser degree). The objective of Oil Depletion Protocol is very simple: to reduce national and global oil dependency. This is in everyone's interest, given the fact that supplies will begin to dwindle at some point in any case, and many years of transition effort will be required in order to avert resulting economic turmoil. But the rate at which this transition *can* be accomplished is understandably proportional to the size of any nation's existing oil-dependent infrastructure: countries that are more dependent now will have more work to do and will require more time to achieve zero petroleum dependency. Thus to demand proportionally *faster* reductions from more-dependent economies than from less-dependent economies is unrealistic.

Further, the Oil Depletion Protocol recognizes that oil dependency is itself a problem (not just the emissions from the burning of oil or other fossil fuels). Thus encouraging more dependency on the part of less-developed nations yields them no long-term benefit—even though they might be able to derive economic growth from using more oil for a short time. If they have proportionally more access to fossil fuels than other nations, they are likely to use those fuels to build more of a fossil-fuel dependent infrastructure, which will almost immediately become problematic once global oil flows peak and there is less available for everyone—less-industrialized nations included. While it is true that some nations have benefited economically from a greater use of fossil fuels until now, thus helping to create enormous global economic inequity, it would be a mistake to attempt to redress that inequity at this time, as Peak Oil and climatic crisis loom, by granting preferential access to hydrocarbon fuels to the countries that appear to have been left behind. A better way to help those nations would be to provide them with open access to new renewable energy technologies (by, for example, waiving intellectual property rights for the development and use of renewable energy technologies domestically) and subsidies for their adoption.

FEASTA's approach—which attempts to solve at once a series of global crises (climate change, economic inequity, the less-industrialized nations' debt crisis, and Peak Oil)—is admirable, and currency reform will indeed be essential to maintaining global economic stability following the oil peak. However, the downside of attempting to solve all of these problems with a single plan is that if that particular plan is not adopted (perhaps due to opposition by the nations that use the largest amounts of fossil fuels, who would have to reduce hydrocarbon emissions proportionally much faster than other nations), then nothing at all might be accomplished.

Therefore just because the Oil Depletion Protocol does not address all of the global problems that need attention, this does not mean that its contribution is unnecessary or unimportant. We must make progress where we can, and the Oil Depletion Protocol would offer tangible benefits for *all* nations, even if it left other work yet to be accomplished. Moreover, its implementation would set an example of global cooperation on an important and potentially contentious issue and would buy time for the nations of the world to focus their attention on issues like inequality and debt.

4

Dealing with Diminishing Oil:
Options and Strategies

WHILE A VOLUNTARY AGREEMENT to limit oil production and imports would offer the benefits of lower
and more stable prices and the reduced likelihood of conflict
over remaining supplies, it would also present an enormous
challenge to the economies of participating countries. Of
course, as we have noted repeatedly, the fact of the diminishing availability of oil will have to be faced in any case—
whether proactively or in a series of improvised responses to
escalating crises. So avoiding the economic challenge presented by the Protocol now will simply mean the acceptance
of eventual calamity.

Assuming that the former, clearly preferable course of action is chosen, how can nations adjust internally to using less
oil? As discussed in Chapter 1, most modern societies are
overwhelmingly dependent on oil for transportation, agriculture, and other purposes. How can that dependence be
voluntarily and systematically reduced?

Recommendations along these lines need not be included as provisions of the Oil Depletion Protocol. What follows are merely suggestions aimed to evoke more research and discussion within nations adopting or considering the Protocol. It is extremely unlikely that all nations would benefit from pursuing the same energy transition strategy, because countries vary widely in their overall mix of energy sources, in their access to the various renewable energy resources (such as sun, wind, biomass, and hydroelectricity), and other factors. Thus each nation will need to arrive at a strategy that best fits its particular economic and environmental conditions.

It should be noted that the governments of Sweden and Iceland have taken the lead in establishing official goals of completely ending their nations' petroleum dependence, and other nations such as Cuba have made important strides to reduce oil consumption. These efforts can be replicated or adapted by other nations—and in fact must be, if the world is to respond peacefully to the inevitable peaking of world oil production.

The process of reducing oil dependence will be challenging from an engineering and research and development standpoint as well as from economic and social perspectives. Substantial analysis will have to be undertaken by each nation in order to arrive at a sensible set of strategies. This short chapter can do no more than point to some promising general avenues.

Replacement

The most obvious strategy to deal with diminishing oil will be replacement of petroleum with other fuels. There is unquestionable need for research and investment with regard to such fuels. However, as discussed in Chapter 1, every one of the likely replacements has one or more serious draw-backs. All are currently very limited in quantity and will re-quire considerable time and investment in order to achieve a scale of production equal to a substantial fraction of that of petroleum today, and all entail environmental costs of vari-ous kinds. Let us examine some of the possibilities.

Renewables

Perhaps the biggest problem with substitutes for oil is that they are intended to replace something highly energy-dense and convenient to use. A single gallon (3.8 liters) of gasoline contains about 36 kilowatt-hours of energy. By way of com-parison, a person working hard can exert, on average, roughly 100 watts of power (champion bicycle racers have been measured at over 300 watts)—though much less if only the power of arm-muscles is counted. Thus a gallon of gas-oline is the energetic equivalent of several weeks of human labor.

This is a degree of energy density that is difficult to match with renewable sources of energy—that is, energy harvested from the natural environment in approximately real time. Most renewable energy originates in sunlight, and the aver-age annual solar incidence at latitude 35 degrees is approxi-mately 1900 kW per square horizontal meter (not a bad average figure to use for the world as a whole). This may seem like a large number, given that the planet has a surface area of over five quadrillion square meters. However, mak-ing use of that energy on an industrial scale presents an enor-mous challenge, because sunlight must be collected and concentrated before it can be used, and that process itself re-quires energy.

Green plants are nature's solar energy collectors and have

evolved over hundreds of millions of years to, with maximum biological efficiency, transform sunlight chemically into carbohydrates. Nevertheless, green plants capture solar energy with only one percent efficiency. In fact, globally, all of green nature collects and concentrates only about ten times as much energy as humans currently obtain from all energy sources. (The total biomass primary energy capture worldwide is 4000 quadrillion Btus, or quads, per year; humans currently use over 400 quads). Thus current world energy needs could conceivably be accommodated by what the biosphere provides, but that assumes essentially no growth in energy usage, no margin for error or significant losses in processing, and little or no regard for preserving habitat for other species.

It is not hard to understand why fossil fuels provide energy so much more cheaply and abundantly than do biological sources. After all, oil was produced from plant material (mostly algae and plankton) that covered seas and lakes collecting sunlight over periods of millions of years; this material was then buried and chemically transformed. According to the calculations of Jeffrey Dukes of the University of Massachusetts Boston, each gallon (4.5 liters) of gasoline we use today represents about a hundred tons of ancient plants slowly cooked over tens of millions of years.[1] Granted, modern methods of biofuels production are more efficient than nature's slow means of producing crude oil, but still this analysis should give us pause: trying to replace a substantial fraction of our 85 million barrels per day of global oil consumption with biofuels could potentially overwhelm agricultural systems already destroying topsoil and drawing down ancient aquifers unsustainably.

Renewable biofuels such as ethanol, wood methanol, and biodiesel are well suited to running existing gasoline, diesel, and perhaps even jet engines. The main drawback is their requirement for arable land for growing crops such as corn, sugar cane, or rapeseed, and hence the inevitability of an eventual trade-off between food and fuel. Paul Mobbs, in *Energy Beyond Oil,* offers an analysis of the land requirements for biodiesel production in the UK, which can be extrapolated to a certain extent for other nations:

> Intensively produced rapeseed yields 3.1 te/ha (tonnes per hectare), or 41.3 GJ/ha of energy. If we take a diesel car that travels 45 miles per gallon, that's an energy expenditure of 0.0048 GJ per mile. So one hectare of land will fuel a diesel car for 8,697 miles. Or, if the average car travels 9,000 miles per year, each car would use 1.03 hectares of land per year (or roughly two and a half acres per year). Scaling up, the 50,000 hectares of rapeseed high in erucic acid that are grown in the UK would support just 48,800 diesel cars for one year. The UK's entire rapeseed crop, 357,000 hectares in 2002, if grown as rapeseed high in erucic acid would keep just 348,000 cars on the road for a year. This assumes that the same high intensity cultivation can continue in the future. If we reduce the fertiliser inputs then the yield would drop to 2.9 te/ha, and the quality of the oil drops so it takes 3 te of rapeseed to produce 1 te of biodiesel. In this case the average car would require 1.17 ha of land per year instead of 1.02 ha/year.[2]

A matter of some controversy is the energy payback from biofuels—that is, whether they require more energy for their production than they yield when burned in vehicle engines.

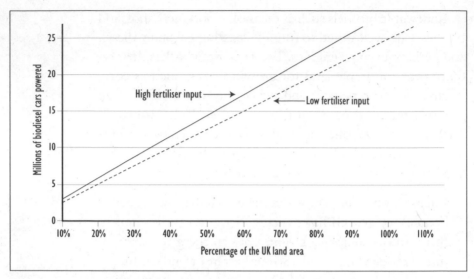

FIGURE 4.1.   Energy production from biodiesel in the UK: the trade-off between crop-land and energy. (CREDIT: Mobbs, *Energy Beyond Oil*.)

Some studies show a net energy loss for ethanol production,[3] while others indicate a net energy gain, at least for some crops.[4]

A study by scientists at UC Berkeley published in *Science* January 27, 2006 claimed to settle the long-standing controversy, concluding that there is indeed a useful energy payback from ethanol, but that greenhouse gas reduction (at least in the case of corn ethanol) is marginal.[5] The authors indicated also that the future for ethanol from sources other than corn (e.g., cellulosic ethanol) is very bright. In an editorial accompanying the study, BP chief scientist Steven Koonin wrote that increased use of biofuels could supplant oil imports, reduce greenhouse gas emissions, and support agriculture. Biofuels, in Koonin's words, could "supply some 30 percent of global demand (for transportation fuels) in an environmentally responsible manner without affecting food production."[6]

However, that assessment may be overly optimistic, according to a reply article by Tad Patzek, also of UC Berkeley. He argues there that the Ferrell study was seriously flawed, and that the energy balance from ethanol production (including cellulosic sources), is indeed low or negative.[7]

There is an old saying, "The grain is for the farmer and the straw is for the land." The point, as every farmer knows, is that one cannot remove all of the production from a field or forest every year without seeing declines in soil fertility. Currently it is possible to remove all production and replace lost nitrogen with chemical fertilizers made from fossil fuels. But it might be a perilous mistake to assume that this strategy can be continued into the indefinite future, much less that it can be expanded sustainably to produce a significant supply of biofuels in addition to food. We will return to the subject of agriculture later in this chapter.

Experience in Thailand with the increased use of biofuels already underscores some of the potential difficulties and tradeoffs. Because rising oil prices were creating problems for the economy of that country, in 2004 and 2005 the government encouraged the use of ethanol made from sugar cane, molasses, and cassava as an extender in gasoline to make gasohol. Such was the demand that domestic supplies could not keep up, as shortages ensued from the competing demands for food and fuel. Three ethanol plants had to close, and construction of 18 more was delayed.[8]

From an energy standpoint it is far more efficient to convert biomass directly to electricity (by burning it close to where it is grown, boiling water for steam turbines) than to convert it into ethanol. The only real advantage of the latter is that it provides a fuel usable in existing vehicles.

In sum, even in the best instance the energy profit from biofuels production is always likely to be small as compared to the energy payback from hydroelectric power or wind turbines, and smaller still when compared to the historic yields from extracting oil and natural gas. While ethanol and biodiesel may prove essential for running some farm machinery and emergency vehicles (as discussed below in the section on agriculture), the prospect of running a substantial portion of the world's fleet of 700,000,000 cars and trucks on biofuels seems extremely remote.

Solar photovoltaic, active solar thermal, wind, tidal, hydro, wave, and geothermal technologies all produce electricity (passive solar thermal and geothermal can also produce heat energy and hot water for buildings). Thus most renewable energy sources other than biofuels will be suitable for running only electric vehicles, unless investment is directed toward the creation of a sizeable infrastructure for using electricity to produce an energy-carrying medium such as hydrogen (more on that below).

Other Fossil Fuels

Because of renewables' inherent limitations, the most competitive energy replacements for oil from an energy standpoint are likely to be other fossil fuels—coal, natural gas, tar sands, kerogen (also known as oil shale), and so on. But of course these other fossil fuels share oil's drawbacks—the fact that burning them releases greenhouse gases, and the fact that they are non-renewable and thus depletable within historic time frames. Moreover, few of the other fossil fuels start out with an energy density comparable to oil's; and transforming coal, tar sands, or kerogen into liquids only reduces their overall energetic payoff, even if the resulting fuels are, in themselves, similar to petroleum in their energy characteristics.

Technologies for transforming natural gas into liquid fuel are currently used to produce fewer than a million barrels per day globally. While building more production facilities could increase this rate, natural gas is already needed for home heating, electricity generation, and fertilizer and chemicals production.

Similarly, technologies for turning coal into a liquid fuel currently produce far fewer than a million barrels per day worldwide. In order to replace a significant portion of petroleum currently consumed globally with liquids from coal would require a dramatic increase in coal mining investment and infrastructure, with an even more dramatic probable increase in greenhouse gas emissions. For these reasons and others discussed in Chapter 1, the effort to scale up CTL production seems unlikely to gain much ground.

Nuclear

Nuclear fuel is even more energy dense than fossil fuels: a single kilogram of uranium can produce an astounding 500,000 kilowatt-hours of electricity—though this is true only of uranium that has been purified through an energy-intensive process, not of raw ore, which has a typical energy density of 100 kWh per kilogram or less. Mining uranium also consumes energy, and is environmentally disruptive.

Nuclear power stations cannot directly replace oil because they produce electricity, not liquid transportation fuels. Over the longer term this problem could be solved by using elec-

tricity to produce an energy carrier capable of running vehicles—most likely hydrogen (again, more on that below).

Moreover, the construction of nuclear power plants is expensive and nuclear fuel is becoming more costly with time.
As energy consultant Mycle Schneider has pointed out:

> The nuclear industry is not even in a position to maintain
> the number of operating plants in the world. As we have
> shown in a recent report, the average age of the operating
> power plants is 21 years. We have assumed an average life-
> time of 40 years for all operating reactors. Considering
> the fact that the average age of all 108 units that already
> have been closed is equally about 21 years, the doubling of
> the operational lifetime seems rather optimistic. The exer-
> cise enables an evaluation of the number of plants that
> would have to come on-line over the next decades in order
> to maintain the same number of operating plants.
> Roughly 80 reactors would have to be planned, built, and
> started up over the next ten years—one every month and a
> half—and an additional 200 units over the following 10-
> year period—one every 18 days. Even if Finland and
> France build a European Pressurized Water Reactor
> (EPR) and China went for an additional 20 plants and
> Japan, Korea, or Eastern Europe added one plant, the
> overall trend will be downwards. With extremely long
> lead times of 10 years and more—the last unit to come on-
> line in the US took 23 years to build—it is practically im-
> possible to maintain or even increase the number of
> operating nuclear power plants over the next 20 years, un-
> less operating lifetimes could be substantially increased
> beyond 40 years on average, simultaneously raising sig-

nificant safety issues. There is currently no basis for such an assumption. In fact, the Lithuanian reactor Ignalina-1, which was shut down on 31 December 2004, remains exactly on world average at age 21.[9]

Schneider concludes that "The relevance of nuclear power for the supply of commercial primary energy to the world is marginal" and that "Nuclear power is most likely on its way out."

While Schneider's conclusions are not shared by many supporters of the nuclear industry, nevertheless most knowledgeable observers of the situation would agree that the replacement of oil with nuclear power presents tremendous obstacles in the forms of enormous investment requirements and the need for the development and deployment of new technologies on an unprecedented scale and with breathtaking speed.

Hydrogen

In recent years many energy futurists have discussed the prospect of a "hydrogen economy." As the world moves away from using fossil fuels, the replacement sources are likely to be varied—including wind, solar, tidal, nuclear, hydro, and biomass—with most of them producing electricity. Moreover, many renewable energy sources are intermittent, thus requiring some means of energy storage. Meanwhile the world's transportation fleet will require an energy carrier capable of making energy from electricity available to run vehicles.

In principle, hydrogen could both store energy produced

as electricity from nuclear or renewable sources (using electricity to split water into oxygen and hydrogen) and provide a fuel for cars and trucks. Hydrogen is non-polluting, produces no greenhouse gases when burned, and has a higher energy density by weight than any of the fossil fuels.[10]

However, a hydrogen economy would entail the construction of an enormous replacement energy infrastructure, with new technology required for production, storage, distribution, and end use.

Producing hydrogen through electrolysis is relatively expensive compared to production from fossil fuels (most commercially produced hydrogen is today made from natural gas), though in principle electricity from wind could yield hydrogen at a cost comparable to that of gasoline today.

While hydrogen has a high energy density per unit of weight, it has a much lower energy density by volume. A gallon of gasoline actually contains much more hydrogen than does a gallon of liquid hydrogen, due to hydrogen's diffuseness even when pressurized or liquefied. This leads to problems with transport and storage. For example, a hydrogen distribution system that attempted to mimic most nations' current gasoline distribution systems would require up to twenty times as many delivery trucks to transport an amount of fuel with the same quantity of energy.[11]

Hydrogen generation and storage systems and fuel cell technologies all deserve more research funding and will no doubt play a role in the world's energy future, but we should not imagine that hydrogen will be able to replace oil on a large scale any time soon. A 2004 report from the US National Academies of Science, titled "The Hydrogen Economy: Opportunities, Costs, Barriers, and R&D Needs," summarizes the situation well in saying that, "In the best case scenario, the transition to a hydrogen economy would take many decades, and any reductions in oil imports and carbon dioxide emissions are likely to be minor during the next 25 years."[12]

Altogether, how much of our current oil consumption can we expect to replace using the available alternatives? The answer will depend partly on the levels of investment provided, and partly on how much time remains to begin the energy transition before oil production peaks. If the peak is soon, the result might be an economic environment in which it would be difficult for nations or industries to make large investments in alternative energy sources. Based on the information presented above, it seems prudent to assume that, even with the best decisions and high levels of investment, it is unlikely that replacement fuels can be made available in sufficient quantity over a reasonable time frame (two decades or less) to supplant likely declines in oil flows. Therefore for the remainder of this chapter we will emphasize and explore response strategies that focus on demand reduction to balance the energy equation.

At the risk of being repetitive, we will again emphasize the point: we are not saying that investments in replacement fuels *should not* be made, merely that strategies to curtail non-essential energy usage and to use energy more efficiently will be cheaper, and will be necessary in any case. No one doubts that some demand-reduction strategies will be difficult and in many cases unpopular, but in the end they will be unavoidable. The sooner they are undertaken, the less disruptive their impacts are likely to be.

Personal Transportation

As discussed in Chapter 2, the personal transportation sector is the largest consumer of petroleum for most (if not all) industrialized countries. With implementation of the Oil Depletion Protocol, oil supplies in signatory nations will controllably contract, strongly impacting transportation and requiring immediate—or, for best effect, pre-emptive—short-term response as well as long-term adjustment in transportation options.

A recent publication of the International Energy Agency (IEA), "Saving Oil in a Hurry," illuminates the costs and benefits associated with short-term transportation sector responses to a reduced oil supply in OECD countries.[13] The report offers guidance primarily with regard to demand reduction in crisis situations, but many of its recommendations might also serve as short-term responses during the initial stages of post-peak oil production declines—or pre-peak planned dependency reduction coordinated by the Oil Depletion Protocol—provided that long-term planning to reduce demand accompanies implementation of these short-term measures.

"Saving Oil in a Hurry" divides transportation crisis response policies into two classes: those that provide fuel-efficient travel options in addition to driving, and those that restrict existing fuel-intensive travel options. Both can yield reductions in fuel demand. Restrictive policies tend to produce greater reductions, but often carry higher political costs arising from public inconvenience.

Policies that increase the number of travel choices available offer a side benefit in the form of greater elasticity of fuel demand. With more options available, more people can, for example, choose to ride commuter rail to work rather than drive when fuel prices get too high. As fuel demand becomes

Oil-saving effects of policies summed across all IEA countries:
Potential Oil Savings by Category Measure

VERY LARGE (more than one million barrels per day)
Carpooling: large program to designate emergency carpool lanes along all motorways, designate park-and-ride lots, inform public and match riders. Cost: Less than $1 per barrel saved.
Driving ban: odd/even license plate scheme. Provide police enforcement, appropriate information and signage—some more privileged drivers can get around driving ban by owning multiple cars. May have diminishing effect over time as drivers adapt. Cost: less than $1 per barrel saved.
Speed limits: reduce highway speed limits to 90km/hr. Provide police enforcement or speed cameras, appropriate information and signage—dependent on adequate enforcement. Cost: less than $10 per barrel saved.

LARGE (more than 500 thousand barrels per day)
Transit: free public transit (set fares to zero). Very costly, inefficient use of funds due to windfall to existing riders. Cost: more than $100 per barrel saved.
Telecommuting: large program, including active participation of businesses, public information on benefits of telecommuting, minor investments in needed infrastructure to facilitate. Relatively cheap, minor political costs. Cost: less than $1 per barrel saved.
Telecommuting: Large program with purchase of computers for 50% of participants. Cost: more than $100 per barrel saved.
Compressed work week: program with employer participation and public information campaign. Relatively cheap, minor political costs. Cost: less than $1 per barrel saved.
Driving ban: 1 in 10 days based on license plate, with police enforcement and signage. Cost: less than $10 per barrel saved.

MODERATE (more than 100 thousand barrels per day)
Transit: 50% reduction in current public transit fares. Cost: more than $100 per barrel saved.
Transit: increase weekend and off-peak transit service and increase peak service frequency by 10%—more equitable than fare reduction. Cost: more than $100 per barrel saved
Carpooling: small program to inform public, match riders. Cost: less than $1 per barrel saved.
Tire pressure: large public information program. Relatively cheap, minor political costs. Cost: less than $1 per barrel saved.

SMALL (less than 100 thousand barrels per day)
Bus priority: convert all existing carpool and bus lanes to 24-hour bus priority usage and convert some other lanes to bus-only lanes. Cost: less than $50 per barrel saved.[14]

more elastic, people can respond better to price signals with reduction of demand rather than with fistfights at the gas pump. The key to benefiting from increased fuel demand elasticity associated with additional transit options, though, is having the options in place before a supply crisis occurs. As the IEA authors put it, "There is smaller reduction in consumer surplus and societal welfare when the elasticity of demand is larger. This should therefore be a primary goal of demand restraint measures—to increase the demand responsiveness of the transport sector to fuel price increases and/or supply constraints."[15]

Carpooling

Among the strategies the IEA discusses is the promotion of carpooling:

> With modern computer technology and experience gained (at least in the United States) at running carpooling programs, it is likely these could be set up much more quickly —and many already exist. In any country, setting up a system to help match travelers with others, to help carpools form quickly, could yield important benefits during a supply crisis.[16]

Carpools are currently advantageous for commuters because many highways now have carpool lanes that remain largely free of traffic congestion, and carpools are exempt from tolls on many toll roads and bridges. These advantages have spurred the creation of many different types of carpooling systems, from "casual carpools" to electronically-arranged "instant carpools" to the more traditional employer-sponsored carpool programs.

Casual carpools are perhaps the most interesting recent

car sharing projects.[17] Casual carpools develop when riders and drivers meet at designated locations during commute hours. Riders partner up with drivers on the spot with no pre-planning, so that both may benefit from the advantages of carpooling. The only planning required is to designate meeting locations, and even then a simple sign tacked to a lightpost or fence is often enough. The rush-hour convergence of commuters generally assures that enough drivers and riders will be going in the same direction at the same time to necessitate no further planning. Casual carpool locations tend to be near public transit hubs, so that riders who miss a ride can still get where they need to go.

Mutually agreed-upon rules also help the system to function smoothly without need for government oversight. The general rules for San Francisco Bay Area casual carpools are as follows: as carpool lanes usually require three or more people per car, casual carpools tend to consist of only three people even if the car will hold a greater number, so that as many drivers as possible can benefit from carpooling. The policy of three people per car also helps to reassure new riders that the system is safe, as there will usually be two riders to every driver. Rides are given on a first-come, first-served basis, and riders form lines to better organize pickups. Money is never given nor asked—rides are offered and taken purely for mutual benefit. Finally, riders are generally silent throughout the ride unless the driver initiates a conversation. Passengers are also always free to decline a ride for any reason, including feeling unsafe with the driver.

Car Co-ops
A citywide car co-op (such as City Car Share in the San Francisco Bay Area, Flexcar in Portland, or the CAN Car coopera-

tive car network in Vancouver, Canada) might offer more transport options during the transition away from petroleum. Car co-ops still entail the personal use of automobiles, but each car, rather than being owned by one driver, is instead part of a fleet shared among many members. Hence fewer cars are needed to serve the transport needs of a given pool of drivers. Insurance, repairs, and other costs are paid for with membership and with hourly and mileage fees. Costs for membership tend to be far lower than the cost of owning a personal vehicle; meanwhile, costs to the environment and city in pollution road damage are reduced, and the total number of cars on the road declines. Car co-ops, like more traditional mass transit, operate best as networks of hubs for pick-up and drop-off. Like mass transit, car co-ops tend to require dense development for effective use.

The organization Community Solution in Yellow Springs, Ohio has created a variation on the car co-op or organized carpool that it terms "Community Car." This proposal would use existing personal transportation, cell phone, and GPS technology, and would adapt software from airline and rental car reservation systems as well as military command-and-control communication systems. The result would be a network of drivers and riders, as well as police and emergency personnel, who could respond, while in transit, to each other's needs. Given a broad enough user base, a rider thus networked could maintain the mobility necessary for the modern industrialized-world lifestyle. The rider could conceivably travel from an outlying suburb to work in one carpool, go from work to a lunch meeting in another, arrange another carpool for an unanticipated pickup of the kids from school, catch another carpool to the store on the way home, and then catch yet another carpool from the store to home.[18]

RideNow, a San Francisco Bay Area innovation on the carpool concept, like Ride Share, already employs information technology to link riders and drivers into instant carpools. Riders use the Web-based software or call in to the phone system to request a ride, while drivers do the same to offer a ride. The system does require drivers and riders to place their requests before they wish to meet up, and then to wait for notification of ride matches. RideNow works in conjunction with public transit to connect commuters in otherwise transit-inaccessible areas with transit hubs.[19]

Many employers and counties around the Bay Area offer "Guaranteed Ride Home," a program designed to soothe carpool riders' worries about being stranded without a ride. The program uses taxis or rental cars to provide regular carpool or transit riders with a free ride home in the event of an emergency. Eligibility and details for the program vary with the organization providing the benefit.[20]

Community-Supported Hitchhiking

Hitchhiking is a practice that predates automobiles and is common throughout most of the world. While an expansion of hitchhiking would result in saved fuel, many potential hitchhikers and driving ride-sharers are deterred by concerns for safety, reliability of service, and privacy. Nevertheless, informal networks to promote the practice have emerged in many places — such as Washington, D.C.'s Virginia suburbs, where drivers, looking for enough passengers to drive in freeway high-occupancy-vehicle (HOV) lanes, have been giving lifts to strangers since the 1980s.

Palo Alto, California transportation consultant Steve Raney has proposed a scheme called "digital hitchhiking" that he says would let people who live near major thorough-

fares catch rides to work without the uncertainty of traditional hitchhiking or the rigidity of organized car pools, using transponders, the Internet, and cell phones to connect
with co-workers driving through the neighborhood on their
way to work. When a prospective hitchhiker who lives in a
particular area is ready to leave home, she will contact a
server through her home computer or by cell phone. In turn,
the server will send a text message with estimates of when the
next few hitchhiker-friendly cars are likely to arrive at her preferred pickup point. Drivers and passengers will hook up at
designated zones. Hitchhikers can walk or bike there—all the
drivers' cars will have bike racks. At work, hitchhikers will use
their office PCs to arrange rides home.[21]

The small Marin County, California community of San
Geronimo's "Go Geronimo" program began registering
prospective hitchhikers and drivers willing to pick them up
in 1997, and designated official hitchhiking stops along the
town's main road.[22] While hitchhiking has since largely been
replaced by a shuttle bus, the program is innovative and is
replicable elsewhere. Both drivers and riders obtain photo
ID laminates, and all adults registered with the program are
required to pass a criminal background check. Participants
simply display their laminate at a designated stop until a car
pulls over, check the driver's "Go Geronomo" registration
number, ask where the driver is going, and declare their destination. There is never an obligation to give or receive a ride.

Transportation: Long-Term Measures

Since automobiles are among the least energy-efficient
means of transportation available, the goal of all nations
must be to reduce automobile use to a minimum. From the
standpoint of energy efficiency alone, it is clear that the best

modes of transportation are human-powered vehicles, such as bicycles, and walking. However, between the efficiency extremes of automobiles and bicycles there exist many intermediary alternatives; moreover, bicycles and walking will not suffice for long-distance transportation or the hauling of heavy cargo.

For travel between cities, industrialized nations have increasingly relied on air transport. However, air travel is approximately as inefficient as travel by automobile, and is thus bound to become more expensive and less affordable as oil prices rise. The obvious long-term replacement for air transport would be increasing reliance on transport by rail and ship, both of which enjoy much higher fuel efficiencies. In the case of trains, there is the option, at least for relatively short routes, of operation by electric rather than diesel motors.

However, the transition away from air transport will be problematic. High ticket prices will tend to reduce non-essential air travel, but will have adverse impacts on tourism and related industries. And in countries such as the US and Canada, where the existing passenger rail infrastructure is incapable of absorbing a substantial increase in riders, considerable time and investment will be required for capacity building.

Within cities there are several options for transport modes between the automobile at one extreme and the bicycle at the other; these primarily consist of alternative-fuel buses, electric buses, surface electric light rail (trolleys), and electric subways, though several imaginative new kinds of transit systems have been proposed.[23] All of these will likewise require time and investment for their installation or expansion.

It is recommended that nations and municipalities:

- Immediately reconsider all planned highway construction.
- Reallocate highway construction monies to developing transportation that is less oil-dependent, especially electrified rail and light rail.
- Give greater priority to walking and cycling in transport and land use planning and transport funding.
- Review and alter taxation measures that encourage car commuting.
- Encourage employer provision of public transport fares and bicycles rather than car and parking options.

Transport users do not pay the real costs of travel, since many costs—such as the health effects of air pollution—are imposed on the community. This mismatch results in social and economic costs for the community and a strain on public funds. Incorporating real costs more fully in what transport users pay would both help influence travel behavior and also provide funds to build more energy-efficient transportation infrastructure. The following are some measures that would help in this regard:

- Change motor vehicle registration charges from fixed payments to payment based on kilometers traveled and vehicle type.
- Remove taxation measures that encourage motor vehicle use and the purchase of four-wheel drives and six-cylinder vehicles over more efficient vehicles.
- Explore implementing road user charges.
- Model oil supply and price scenarios to inform local debate about the economic and social implications of transport options.

Urban Design

Since the use of liquid fuels for transportation constitutes such a large share of world petroleum demand, controlled adjustment to declining oil supplies will necessarily incorporate the transformation, shrinking, and elimination of many aspects of modern transportation systems. As we have seen, part of such a strategy would be to increase public transit availability and connectivity; but since transportation needs are so directly tied to land-use patterns, a complete rethinking of modern settlement planning, including both the built landscape and the laws that shape it, must also be undertaken.

For the time being, the nature of existing settlement patterns will constrain choices regarding mass-transit systems: for economic viability, for bus systems to provide service every 10 minutes an urban density of 15 houses per acre (.4 hectare) is required; light rail requires about 9 homes per acre or 19 million square feet (1.77 million square meters) of retail space.[24] Suburban areas characterized by low-density housing will thus present problems for mitigating the effects of diminishing oil supplies—hence the need to address urban-design considerations as soon and quickly as possible.

Settlements that require the least transportation energy tend to be walkable and public-transit oriented, meaning that they are dense, with multiple households living in close proximity. Apartment houses and boarding houses, as well as roommate arrangements, typify walkable design. Walkable

Steps to shrinking the car culture and expanding a transit culture:
- Rezone urban areas for mixed use
- Rezone for density and central hubs
- Take out damaging roads
- Emphasize intermodal transit
- Price private transport at true cost
- Apply extra money to subsidizing public transit infrastructure, to make up for years of damage from competition with car culture.

(Distilled from *Asphalt Nation* by Jane Holtz Kay, Crown, 1997)

settlements are also diverse in their uses, and include residential, commercial, and other uses in close proximity. Ideally, residents of such neighborhoods can in less than ten minutes walk from home to work, school, or a store, or to a transit stop that will take them to one of these destinations. To encourage neighborhoods such as these, building codes must allow for dense, mixed-use settlement.

For years, city planners have thought that dense neighborhoods with little parking and narrow streets simply led to traffic gridlock. But experience shows that smart, compact development actually reduces, rather than clogs, car traffic, resulting in more walking and transit use and less demand for fuel.[25] A dense and diverse neighborhood, like a well-established natural system, encourages activity beneficial to the system; a city built of such neighborhoods discourages the cancer-like overgrowth of highway-oriented, low-density strip development and the resulting death of the city center. Many planners have already begun to see the sense of designing for people rather than cars, and many municipalities already incorporate urban-growth boundaries and targets for residential density increases in their strategies to halt sprawl and better integrate land use and transport. The New Urbanist SmartCode is one policy approach to planning for walkability.[26]

Developers build in outlying suburban areas because the land is cheap, and customers buy homes in suburban areas because the homes are affordable. However, many people would prefer to live in cities were it not for the higher home prices in many existing high-density urban neighborhoods. The cost of owning or renting in the city shows the popularity of denser living. Densification of existing settlements through infill development can provide both the dense living and affordable housing that people need.

As planners begin to understand the benefits of walkability, and the thrust of new development is redirected from suburban car-centered spaces into dense pedestrian-centered spaces, there remains the problem of how to curb further growth and deal with existing car-centered design. Application of the principles of density and diversity to defunct city centers can revitalize cities previously gutted in the last century's mass exodus to the suburbs. Infill development has reclaimed many neighborhoods already, and could provide much more low-cost, low-energy, walkable living space. There is also some precedent for dismantling existing roads that citizens determine are damaging their community. In downtown Providence, Rhode Island, officials restored the Woonasquatucket River and created a public space that helped to revitalize their downtown by removing the acres of highway that covered the river.[27] On a more personal scale, large homes can be converted into flats and rented out, or (as is already the common practice of college students and singles in many cities) individual rooms can be rented out.

Public transit works in concert with walkable design. Density and diversity of use create the necessary environment for a successful public transit system, while a healthy transit system creates an environment for dense and diverse living. Designers need to consider both if the urban system is to sustain itself. Good public transit should also mesh into its community with an ample number of intermodal transit options: walking or bicycling should bring the traveler easily to bus or light rail stops, which should connect to rapid transit hubs and commuter rail hubs, which should connect to regional rail.

EcoCity designer and author Richard Register writes:

Priorities for urban design should be: first pedestrian access, then bicycles, then elevators, then streetcars and trains, then buses, and last cars—and probably only for emergencies and rental for travel to remote areas far from cities. Without the realization that the pedestrian city is possible, design can get tangled in massive contradictions, such as in promoting the energy-efficient car—which in fact most efficiently promotes sprawl and the inefficient city. The city based on ecological principles can then be designed as a pedestrian/dense and diverse/renewable energy infrastructure taking up far less land than is the case with the car/sprawl city. For those who think it's impossible, there are the examples of Venice, Italy; Zermatt, Switzerland; the Medina at Fez; and Gulongyu, China. Anything that exists is possible and those four are all car-free cities that definitely exist. They also thrive.[28]

According to Register, the the most ecologically healthy cities are likely to be roughly seven times as dense as car/sprawl cities, though we will not know that ratio with more precision until more such cities are built. We do know that two lines of rail equal sixteen lanes of freeway in delivering passengers or freight. Clearly, designing cities for the post-petroleum future will yield many side benefits along the way.

Agriculture

As noted previously, modern agriculture's overwhelming dependence on petroleum constitutes one of the world's most important vulnerabilities to Peak Oil. To see how we might go about reducing this vulnerability, we need first to understand how oil is being used in the current global food system, and then explore how we can reduce the amount of petroleum consumed while maintaining food production at or near current levels.

Fertilizer and the Problem of Soil Fertility

Most fossil fuel used in modern agriculture is not pumped into gas tanks, but instead sprayed onto fields in the form of water-soluble fertilizer. Nitrogen fertilizer, made from natural gas, accounts for 47 percent of total energy usage for corn farming in the American Midwest; percentages for other crops and nations vary, but remain substantial in most cases compared to other energy inputs. (While reducing usage of natural gas for this purpose is not directly relevant to our discussion of petroleum, it has indirect relevance as natural gas is also a depleting fuel, and freeing up natural gas supplies could assist in oil replacement strategies.)

Chemical fertilizers quickly leach out of the soil or run off into nearby waterways, necessitating repeated applications and causing productivity losses in nearby aquatic systems. Artificial fertilizers, particularly nitrogen,

Total energy requirements of farm inputs for nine-State and nine-State weighted average, 2001.[29] Data is for corn production in IL, IN, IA, MN, NE, OH, MI, SD, and WI, weighted average.

	BTU/bushel	Percentage of Total
Seed	603	1.2%
Fertilizer		
Nitrogen	23477	47%
Potash	1899	3.8%
Phosphate	1631	3.3%
Lime	63	.01%
Energy		
Diesel	7491	15%
Gasoline	3519	7.0%
LPG	2108	4.2%
Electricity	2258	4.5%
Natural Gas	1846	3.7%
Custom Work	1581	3.2%
Chemicals	2941	5.9%
Purchased Water	136	.03%
Input Hauling	202	.04%
Total	49753	98.88%

(some error due to rounding)

also stimulate soil bacteria—the engines that drive sustained soil fertility—to consume their food source: carbon-rich organic matter, or soil humus. Humus helps soils to hold onto mineral and other nutrients and supports a varied ecology of soil bacteria. Due to past patterns of over-reliance on artificial fertilizers and soil tillage, over half of the humus in most temperate-climate soils is gone. Because of the lack of humus and the consequently simplified soil ecology, much of the world's cropland would be largely barren if not for constant petrochemical inputs. Rebuilding soil humus can go a long way toward minimizing the continuing need for fossil fuels in agriculture.

Brown coal might help quickly convert much of the world's now-fossil-dependent conventional farms to organic, low-input farms, sustaining high yields but weaning our food systems off chemical fertilizers. While brown coal is itself a fossil fuel, its use could be justifiable in a transition strategy to jump-start renewable compost-based soil fertility. David Holmgren, one of the originators of the Permaculture movement, writes:

> High-sulfur brown coals are especially valuable because sulfur is a valuable plant nutrient. Coal-based fertilizers are increasingly being used in the conversion of conventional agriculture to organic methods; they offer the hope of building the long-term, stable humus content of soils at a faster rate than is possible with traditional methods. We need to remain cautious about the enduring value of any novel fast track to fertile and balanced soil, given the history of our collective failures. However, using fossil fuel directly to rebuild the natural capital of our farmlands sounds a better bet than burning it for industrial and consumer electricity.[30]

Pest Control

Organic agriculture also has an answer to conventional agriculture's reliance on petroleum-based pesticides and herbicides. Coordinating planting and harvesting dates to avoid pest species population blooms, properly managing soil nutrients and water, intercropping (in which many different species of plants, including food plants and cover crops, are grown closely associated with one another), and releasing pest predators are just some of the ingenious strategies that organic farmers have developed to reduce their crops' exposure to pests. Above all, chemical-free pest management requires close observation of the unique challenges and benefits of each individual site, and human labor to manage them. This suggests that, with declining petroleum availability, the agricultural sector could offer significant growth in employment opportunities.[31]

Farm Machinery: Yields, Energy, and Labor

Energy to run farm machinery can come from biofuels produced on-site. While, as we have seen, there is not enough cropland available for biofuel production to meet the total current liquid-fuel needs of the world, individual farms can benefit from small-scale biofuel production for on-farm use. The average farm in the US uses 8.75 gallons (40 liters) of fuel per acre, while the average canola crop in the US produces 145 gallons (659 liters) of canola oil per acre. A small field of oilcrops could fuel machinery used for other crops, reducing farmers' dependence on petroleum-based liquid fuels. Farmers can process oil into biodiesel easily and cheaply on a small scale, further cutting agricultural energy demand by reducing the amount of energy required to transport fuel to farms.[32]

The thousands of organic farms and gardens that are successfully functioning worldwide demonstrate clearly that agriculture need not be dependent on fossil energy to provide good yields. But agriculture will always require energy. Petroleum-independent food production is labor-intensive, and the mass replacement of fossil energy inputs with renewable ones will require a larger proportion of the population to be directly involved in producing at least some of their own food.[33]

Transportation of Product to Market

Action at all levels of government can help to localize food production. At the international level, given enough pressure from popular movements and the diminishing viability of long-distance transport, governments can renegotiate international trade treaties.

Current trade rules, which encourage the transport of food in larger quantities and further distances, will need to be rethought as energy sources for transportation become more expensive. Such rules, in the view of many, are already harmful; Helena Norberg Hodge, et. al., argue in their book *Bringing the Food Economy Home* that, in less industrialized countries, the cycle of cash cropping, marginalization of the food base, and urbanization of poor subsistence farmers who have been forced off their land must stop. International trade laws that favor international agribusinesses have forced poorer countries to replace traditional farms and fishing industries with cash crops such as cotton, flowers, or luxury foods like farmed shrimp for the global markets. Cash cropping forces traditional local food systems into the margins of society and into the least productive land. A glut of cash crops on the global market follows, sparking off a "race to the bottom" as agribusinesses try to lower overhead costs, maximize output, and stay profitable at the expense of local people everywhere. Industrial, national-scale food systems in all countries join in the race to the bottom in order to stay profitable on the global market. To keep up in the race, developed-world agribusiness invests heavily in production processes that are sparse in workers but intense in petroleum use and that require national subsidies to agribusiness, degrading national food security in the process.[34]

Government subsidies to agriculture currently tend to favor large operations aimed at growing for distant markets. Petroleum-intensive transportation systems that are paid for with government funds also serve to subsidize food systems requiring long-distance transport. In order to reveal and remove the inefficiencies in a food system that requires transport of products over such long distances, these subsidies must be reversed. Small organic farms that grow for local markets are uncompetitive when governments pay for the major costs associated with large global agribusiness, but as the energy to produce and transport food becomes more costly, small organic farms will serve more people more effectively. Reworking the structure of subsidies before energy becomes very scarce will create more food security in the long run.[35]

Assigning Priorities

Altogether, the transition away from petroleum will constitute an immense project for every nation and for the world as a whole. (There are aspects of that transition that we have not touched upon, including the need to reduce usage of, and provide substitutes for, petrochemicals and plastics.)

This project will be costly and will require many years— decades, in fact—of sustained effort. In order to enlist the hard work, cooperation, and creativity of their populations, national governments must educate them about the nature of the energy transition underway, and seek to build consensus around strategic responses to oil scarcity. This educational and consensus-building project must take high priority, must be carried forward with a wartime level of effort, and must be sustained indefinitely. Meanwhile, governments must lead by example, making their own operations as energy-efficient as possible.

Again, this project will be far more easily undertaken if nations can concentrate on it without distraction from the needs of having to compete for remaining oil resources, or of having to adapt to frequent, radical shifts in oil prices.

5

Discussion of the Protocol:
Questions and Objections

W HILE THE OIL DEPLETION PROTOCOL offers fairly obvious potential benefits, nations will naturally seek to probe its potential costs. Its adoption will almost certainly entail a range of implications that are not readily apparent, and so it is important that these be anticipated and considered. We identify and address some likely questions and objections below.

What if forecasts of a near-term peak in global oil production are wrong? Won't there be a cost to preparing for the oil peak too early? In practical terms, won't this mean voluntarily foregoing economic growth?

This is probably the most important criticism likely to be levelled against the Protocol. Because so much is at stake, it is important that this criticism be addressed not just by partisan participants in the debate over the timing of the oil-production peak; some independent assessment is required of the costs of preparing too soon versus the costs of preparing too late.

Fortunately, such an assessment has already been undertaken in the Hirsch Report, discussed in Chapter 1.

The Hirsch Report agrees that mitigation efforts undertaken too soon would exact a cost on society. However, it concludes that, "If peaking is imminent, failure to initiate timely mitigation could be extremely damaging. Prudent risk management requires the planning and implementation of mitigation well before peaking. Early mitigation will almost certainly be less expensive than delayed mitigation."[1]

But what if the peak is more than two decades away? The Hirsch Report concludes that, with two decades of effort in the development of alternative fuels, it would be possible to avert shortfalls of transportation fuel when the peak finally arrives. According the USGS report, "World Petroleum Assessment 2000," we have more than two decades.[2]

Given the fact that so many other studies and reports suggest that the peak may occur much sooner, it would be irresponsible of governments to rely only on the most optimistic estimates of world oil endowment and future production rates. It is the responsibility of governments and policy makers to plan for contingencies. As we have noted, Peak Oil is not a speculative occurrence; it is inevitable. Many analysts argue that it will occur within the next one to seven years. Given these credible forecasts, failure to respond or to prepare would constitute negligence on a monstrous scale.

What if the peak arrives soon and the rate of decline post-peak is greater than 2.6 percent? After all, some nations that are past their national peaks are experiencing production decline rates in the range of five to ten percent per year. Might something like this occur for the world as a whole as well? In that case, wouldn't the Oil Depletion Protocol be ineffectual at preventing price spikes and conflict over remaining supplies?

If the peak occurs soon, and if the Oil Depletion Protocol is adopted, a decline rate higher than 2.5 percent for the world as a whole seems unlikely in the early years, though the rate would likely increase over time as new discoveries (with which to replace existing production) will eventually fall to nearly zero. The Protocol would help keep production declines low by reducing the motivation to pump wells at maximum rates, a practice that reduces the amount ultimately recoverable from those wells, thus leading to steeper decline rates once local production peaks. Also over the near term (approximately the next two decades), non-conventional sources are likely to be brought into production at rates sufficient to help keep decline rates of total hydrocarbon liquids in the one to three percent range.

Nevertheless, this is a valid concern.

The instance in which high decline rates are most likely to occur is one in which the peak is delayed as long as possible by maximum extraction rates supported by all technical means available, and in which the Oil Depletion Protocol is not adopted until after the global peak has already passed. In that instance, once the Protocol is adopted it might be necessary to adjust the world depletion rate upward arbitrarily (no arbitrary adjustment in national depletion rates would be required) to slightly exceed the actual rate of world production decline.

What if the more conservative analysts are right and the world is at its peak of oil production now? In that case, is it too late to implement the Oil Depletion Protocol?

If the world reaches the peak of production within the

next two years there will be too little time to undertake major mitigation efforts prior to the event, and therefore there are likely to be unavoidable economic, social, and political impacts, as outlined in the Hirsch Report.

However, in that case the need for the Protocol should quickly and widely become apparent. While all nations will suffer from higher prices and shortages, only a cooperative system of national and international quotas will avert the even more extreme economic and geopolitical crises that would otherwise ensue.

What if available exports decline faster than total production? An exporter can only export what is left after domestic consumption is satisfied. Consider a simple example, a country producing 2.0 Mb/d, consuming 1.0 Mb/d and therefore exporting 1.0 Mb/d. Assume a 25 percent drop in production over a six year period (which we have seen in the North Sea) and assume a 10 percent increase in domestic consumption. Production would be 1.5 Mb/d. Consumption would be 1.1 Mbpd. Net exports would be production (1.5 Mb/d) minus consumption (1.1 Mb/d) = 0.4 Mb/d. Therefore, because of a 25 percent drop in production and a 10 percent increase in domestic consumption, net oil exports from our hypothetical net exporter drops by 60 percent, from 1.0 Mb/d to 0.4 Mb/d, over a six year period. Under these circumstances, wouldn't prices skyrocket, and competition intensify, even with the Protocol?[3]

This is indeed a matter for concern. If this scenario does play out, the Oil Depletion Protocol will at least help somewhat; then, in order for the agreement to make a significant difference, the World Depletion Rate would have to be adjusted upward arbitrarily, perhaps to three, four, or even five percent per year. This would pose an enormous economic challenge to importing nations, but they would still be much better off with the Protocol than without it.

How would signatory countries actually go about reducing imports?

This could be done very simply through import quotas, which have a long history—usually for the purpose of protecting domestic producers of a specific commodity from foreign competition. In this case, the quotas would of course serve a different function.

In nations where oil is imported by a single state-owned company, the process would be relatively simple, but it would still require long-range planning in order to minimize seasonal shortfalls. In nations where many private companies import oil, the government could auction off import quotas on either a yearly or a monthly basis and thereby raise revenue that could be used, for example, to help fund the building of public transportation infrastructure.

Wouldn't such import quotas violate the rules of the World Trade Organization (WTO)?

These quotas would, as mentioned, serve an entirely different function from the protectionist import quotas that are typically targeted by the WTO. It is therefore to be hoped that the WTO would explicitly allow them.

In any case, the WTO would not challenge the provisions of the Oil Depletion Protocol directly. That institution's role is to adjudicate complaints filed by member nations. Thus a complaint would have to be filed in order to trigger WTO action.

There are two categories of likely complainants: oil-exporting nations unable to find a sufficient market for their product and desirous of higher prices, and oil-importing nations wanting to increase their share of the available world exports.

Let us look at the situation from the perspectives of each of these categories of nations. Why would they wish, or not wish, to file complaints?

Exporters: Today few oil-exporting nations are able to increase their rate of production substantially. OPEC has virtually abolished its export quotas, and nearly all non-OPEC exporting nations are producing at maximum rates. Those exporting nations that have *not* ratified the Protocol will feel no threat from the actions of those that have; quite the contrary: the actions of signatory exporters will make it easier for non-signatory exporters to expand production if they are able to do so, as the former's production restraint will result in less oil being available on the export market. However, non-signatory exporters might be negatively impacted by the actions of signatory importers, whose import restraint will reduce the world demand for oil and thereby reduce upward pressure on prices. But are non-signatory exporting nations likely to take a complaint to the WTO to force markets open and raise prices, when to do so would negatively impact all importers? Here analysis ends and pure speculation begins.

Importers: From the perspective of the non-signatory importing nation, if all other importers are abiding by the Protocol there would be only benefits: prices would be low and there might be extra oil available from non-signatory exporters. Non-signatory importing nations might complain to the WTO in order to force signatory exporters to export more, but such a move would likely have no beneficial practical effect, given the fact that most oil-producing nations are facing declining rates of production for purely geological reasons.

How would nations allocate declining oil supplies domestically?

As we saw in Chapter 3, coupon or quota rationing systems can work well, and are usually the best ways of allocating non-luxury resources or goods during times of scarcity. The rationing of oil and perhaps other energy sources by quota internally within nations would avert some of the worst impacts from soaring prices and perhaps provide benefits along the way.

The most promising recent theoretical effort toward designing a workable energy quota system is described in the short book, *Energy and the Common Purpose*, by British writer David Fleming.[4] Fleming calls the proposed units Tradable Energy Quotas, or TEQs.

TEQs can be used to ration all hydrocarbon energy sources (in order to reduce greenhouse gas emissions) or specific fuels such as oil. For the sake of discussion, let us assume the use of TEQs for petroleum only, as a way of implementing the Oil Depletion Protocol within nations.

First, a national Petroleum Budget would be drawn up, based on the nation's indigenous production and oil imports as mandated by the Oil Depletion Protocol. A segment of the Petroleum Budget would then be issued as an unconditional entitlement to all adults and divided equally among them; the remainder would be auctioned to industry, commercial users, and government (as import or production quotas). The units could then be bought and sold, so that users unable to cope with their ration could increase it, while others who kept their fuel consumption low could sell and trade their petro-units on the national market. All transactions would be carried out electronically, using technologies and systems already in place for direct debit systems and credit cards.

When consumers (citizens, businesses, or the government) made purchases of fuel, they would surrender their quotas to the energy retailer, accessing their quota account by using their petro-card or direct debit. The retailer would then surrender the quota units when buying energy from the wholesaler. Finally, the primary energy provider would surrender units back to the National Register when the company pumped or imported the oil. This closes the loop.

All purchases of petroleum would be made with petro-units, whether the oil were used as fuel or as feedstock for plastics or chemicals. So long as the petroleum remained fuel, petro-units would have to be passed back up the line, starting with the end user. However, if the petroleum were incorporated as feedstock into the manufacturing of a product (e.g., plastics), the manufacturer would simply add the cost of the petro-units into the cost of the product. Thus, in the case of feedstocks, the manufacturer of goods would be the presumed end user.

Purchasers not having any petro-units to offer at point of sale—foreign visitors, people who had forgotten their card or cashed-in all their quota as soon as they received it—would buy a quota at point of purchase, then immediately surrender it in exchange for fuel, but would pay a cost penalty for this (i.e., the bid-and-offer spread quoted by the market).

TEQs would place everyone in the same boat: house-

holds, industry, and government would have to work together, facing the same Petroleum Budget, and trading on
the same market for petro-units. Everyone would have a
stake in the system. All would have the sense that their own
efforts at conservation were not being wasted by the energy
profligacy of others, and that the system was fair. Market
mechanisms would still govern distribution, but in a way
that would encourage cooperation and conservation.

Moreover, TEQs are guaranteed to be effective, because
the only fuel that could be purchased would be fuel within
the Budget. The Budget would set a long time-horizon so
that people would have the motivation and information they
needed to take action in the present to achieve drastic reductions in oil use over a 20-year or longer timeframe.

*Why can't the market take care of the problem without need for in-
terventions like the Oil Depletion Protocol and TEQs? Won't high
prices by themselves stimulate more exploration, conservation,
efficiency, and the development of alternatives?*

As discussed in Chapter 1, the Hirsch Report's authors
dismiss the claim that the market will solve any shortage
problems arising from global oil production peak, with
higher oil prices stimulating investments in alternative energy sources, more efficient cars, and so on. Price signals
warn only of immediate scarcity. However, the mitigation
efforts needed in order to prepare for the global oil production peak and thus to head off shortages and price spikes
must be undertaken many years in advance of the event.
Hirsch, *et al.,* maintain that, "Intervention by governments
will be required, because the economic and social implications of oil peaking would otherwise be chaotic. The experi-

ences of the 1970s and 1980s offer important guides as to government actions that are desirable and those that are undesirable...."[5]

But wouldn't interference with market mechanisms be harmful to the natural process of economic adaptation to fuel scarcity? For example, if the Protocol works to keep prices low, wouldn't that have the effect of reducing the incentives to develop alternatives?

It is true that artificially low prices for any given resource usually both deter efforts to use that resource more efficiently and discourage investors from helping develop alternatives. That is why price controls are generally a bad idea.

However, if the Protocol were widely adopted, incentives to develop alternatives and to increase efficiency would still be present because of the reduced supply of available oil. Oil prices would be stable, but high. And there would be a gradually growing demand for alternatives to supply marginal increases in energy to supplement declining oil.

How will adoption of the Protocol affect importers and exporters differently?

Importers: No one doubts that industrial nations will find it difficult to sustain robust economic growth while using less oil on a yearly basis. Thus the voluntary adoption of the Protocol by importers would seem disadvantageous—a "tough sell."

However, it must be recognized, as we have pointed out repeatedly, that a decline in the availability of oil is inevitable in any case; only the timing of the onset of decline is uncertain. Without a structured agreement in place to limit imports, nations will be inclined to put off preparations for the energy transition until prices soar, at which time such a transition will become far more difficult because of the ensuing chaotic economic conditions. With the Protocol in place, importers will be able to count on stable prices and can then more easily undertake the difficult but necessary process of planning for a future with less oil.

Poor importing countries may object that by using less petroleum they will have to forego conventional economic development. However, further development that is based on the use of petroleum will merely create structural dependency on a depleting resource. Without the Protocol, these nations will be financially bled by high and volatile prices. With the Protocol in place and with prices stabilized, these nations will be able to afford to import the oil they absolutely need; meanwhile they will have every incentive to develop their economies in a way that is not petroleum-dependent.

Exporters: Economies that are based primarily on income from the extraction and export of natural resources often tend to give rise to governments that are more responsive to the interests of powerful foreign resource buyers than they are to the needs of their own citizens. Thus it is in the interest of resource-exporting countries to develop indigenous industries in order to diversify their economies.

Countries that depend primarily on income from oil exports will need to wean themselves from this dependence eventually in any case as their oilfields are depleted; the Protocol provides them a means of making the transition in a way that will allow for long-term planning.

Without the Protocol, smaller exporting nations might be at the mercy of militarily powerful importers. The Protocol will provide a means of minimizing external political interference in these nations' affairs. As a result, much international tension and conflict, including the threat of terrorism, can be minimized—which will be a help also to the wealthy importers.

How will the oil companies be affected?

Without the Protocol, the oil companies may enjoy record revenues—for a time. But they will be demonized for profiting from the misery of the rest of society; meanwhile, they will be hampered in their operations by the destabilization of national economies resulting from wildly gyrating oil prices.

Historically, oil production has often been managed by governments or by cartels. In petroleum's early days, free-market boom-and-bust cycles bankrupted many players (including the "father" of the oil industry, Edwin Drake). Soon John D. Rockefeller brought a certain order to the situation through the creation of the Standard Oil Trust; in doing so he squeezed out many competitors and personally profited to an extraordinary degree. This regime came to an end in 1911, when the US Government broke up Standard Oil after prosecution for violation of anti-trust laws. Starting in the 1930s, with the US in position to control global oil prices, the Texas Railroad Commission capped production levels in order to stabilize prices. After US oil production peaked in 1970 and that nation lost its ability to control global prices, petroleum's center of gravity shifted to the Middle East, and OPEC began mandating production quotas for its members in order to keep prices within a desirable band.

The oil companies accepted (sometimes reluctantly) these mechanisms, recognizing that a stable economic environment was more important to them in the long run than the opportunity to make momentary windfall profits.

While the management of oil production globally thus has precedents, the situation in the future will be fundamentally different from that heretofore. Previously the problem was too much oil and collapsing prices that offered little incentive for exploration. The situation the world will soon face is that of insufficient supply leading to extreme price shocks, price volatility, and acute shortages. Thus a new kind of management scheme will be required.

With the Protocol, the oil companies will remain profitable, they will have the incentive to undertake further exploration, and they will be able to plan decades ahead. They will also be motivated to become more generalized energy companies (rather than remaining merely oil companies), by investing in the development of alternative energy sources.

There is already evidence that the oil companies are concerned about a public backlash as gasoline prices soar: in 2004, ChevronTexaco initiated a public-relations campaign titled "Will You Join Us?", featuring a web site (www.willyou joinus.com) and expensive newspaper ads informing readers that "the era of easy oil is over" and asking for public discussion on the issue. The Oil Depletion Protocol will provide more long-term security for the petroleum industry than any PR campaign ever could, and at no cost.

Won't both importers and exporters be tempted to cheat? How would the Protocol be enforced?

Yes, nations could cheat either by producing too much or by importing too much. The Protocol will require a system for monitoring production, exports, and imports—which cannot be hidden to a large degree in any case. Enforcement will require the establishment of a secretariat for adjudication of disputes and claims, and a system of economic penalties to be negotiated by the agreeing nations, as described in Chapter 3.

If a country discovers a new oilfield but decides to abide by the Protocol, what is its depletion rate? Would that country be able to set its depletion rate such that its corresponding production under the Protocol could be as high or low as desired?

An estimate of future discovery would be incorporated into the national depletion rate to begin with, when the country's reserves were surveyed upon signing the Protocol. Thus in all likelihood the depletion rate would stay the same, and production would continue to decline at that rate. In the event of a truly stupendous discovery, the depletion rate would be adjusted downward, enabling that nation to reduce the scale of its production restrictions under the Protocol. The nation would continue to produce *less* oil each year than the year before, but not as much less as would have been the case without the discovery.

Could a nation reduce its production at a rate greater than its national depletion rate?

Yes, and some might be forced to do so, at least in some years, by geology. Others might decide to do so in order to preserve their endowment for the future. However, since most exporters are keen to profit from oil sales and could use the income to fund their energy transition domestically, the strong likelihood is that nearly all exporting countries would produce as much as they were allowed under the Protocol.

What if only a few nations sign on? Won't the Protocol be ineffectual if a few large exporters or importers refuse to do so?

If only a few exporting nations adopt the Protocol, this would not be any discouragement to importers wishing to sign on, nor would it handicap other exporters—either signatories to the agreement or non-signatories.

At first it might seem that those importing nations not adopting the Protocol would achieve an advantage. However, any temporary benefit would be purchased at the expense of later economic calamity. As implied in the Hirsch Report, nations that embark on the energy transition sooner will be much better off than those procrastinating.

Clearly, importers would benefit more from the Protocol if all, or a substantial majority, of other importing nations adopted it, because only general adoption would lead to substantial price stabilization and reduction in competition. But even if only one nation signs on, that nation will benefit by having a framework in place within which to accomplish the inevitable energy transition in an orderly, planned manner.

What about natural gas and coal—should there be similar protocols for these?

As discussed in Chapter 3, the Oil Depletion Protocol will in no way preclude other agreements aimed at reducing fossil fuel usage in order to avoid impacts to the global climate, and a strong Kyoto accord will be essential in tandem with the Oil Depletion Protocol in order to discourage nations from attempting to make up for oil shortfalls by turning to coal or other low-grade fossil fuels—whose climate impacts are even worse than those from burning oil.

If nations' experience with the Oil Depletion Protocol is positive, this will provide motivation for the forging of similar agreements covering other fossil fuels.

Will efforts to adopt the Protocol distract attention and resources from efforts, already under way, to develop local strategies for responding to Peak Oil?

Regional and municipal programs to develop local food and economic systems that are sustainable in the context of dwindling fossil fuel supplies are needed, and are indeed being undertaken in many places as we will describe in Chapter 6. Rather than taking attention away from local efforts, the Protocol will provide a national and international context in which they can succeed. Without the Protocol, such efforts are likely to be overwhelmed by chaotic economic and political developments beyond the control of local communities. With the Protocol, municipalities and regions will have greater incentive to provide public transit options, and to redesign urban areas minimizing the need for private automobiles. Thus local and international efforts to respond to the problem of Peak Oil will bring mutual, simultaneous benefits.

6

How Can the Protocol Be Adopted?

W E HOPE THAT BY THIS POINT we have identified the
benefits that the Oil Depletion Protocol would bring
and the serious harms that it would avert. We hope that we
have also answered the significant objections likely to be levelled against it.

One important question remains: How might nations,
municipalities, and individuals go about adopting or supporting the Protocol?

It would be foolish to overlook the political difficulties inherent in the project of gaining official acceptance of this
simple agreement, but just as foolish to assume that those
difficulties are insurmountable. To be successful, the project
of seeking adoption of the Protocol must be strategic and
sustained. It must offer opportunities for the involvement of
concerned citizens. And it must begin immediately.

The author and the many direct and indirect contributors
to this book are already engaged in efforts to communicate
the Protocol to world leaders.

Dr. Colin Campbell has done the original and essential work of proposing the Protocol and drafting the language of a specific Protocol document that can be adopted by any nation immediately. Over the past several years he has also discussed the Protocol at many conferences.

The Post Carbon Institute, working in concert with several funding organizations, has founded a nonprofit Oil Depletion Protocol Project, which is currently gathering a small staff. The Project's purpose is to promote the Protocol worldwide in every way possible—by making copies of this book (translated into various languages) available to policy makers, by producing and distributing a brief DVD explaining the Protocol, and by undertaking the lobbying effort that will be needed to obtain adoption. We are also seeking to obtain written endorsements of the Protocol from non-governmental organizations and prominent individuals. The Protocol Project welcomes the help—financial and otherwise—of the general public in its efforts. To donate and to find out how to advance our efforts in other ways, please go to the website www.oildepletionprotocol.org.

We recognize that this process will require time. We also recognize that we must seek to educate top-level decision makers not just in government but also in industry, as well as members of the general public, because without pressure from the business community and from the public, government leaders will be unlikely to take the political risk of proposing or supporting the Protocol.

National Efforts

When the first country adopts the Protocol, this will initiate a global discussion about it. Therefore in order that we can focus our efforts strategically, we are seeking to identify which nations are most likely to be early adopters. As mentioned previously, many oil-exporting nations are already experiencing declining rates of production; for these nations, there would be little to lose by agreeing to export less in the future: for reasons of geology, they have no real choice anyway, so why not make a virtue out of necessity?

A few other nations are already acknowledging the need to reduce petroleum dependency for either environmental or national-security reasons. Some of these countries may likewise be among the first to adopt the Protocol.

In December 2005, Swedish Prime Minister Göran Persson acknowledged that the global oil peak is a problem that needs to be addressed now, and announced the appointment of a National Commission on Oil Independence with the objective of making Sweden oil-independent by 2020. The Commission will study mitigation measures and issue a report in summer 2006.[1]

In April 2006 Forfás, Ireland's national board responsible for providing policy advice to Government on enterprise, trade, science, technology, and innovation, released a report titled "A Baseline Assessment of Ireland's Oil Dependence: Key Policy Considerations." This report examines the extent to which the Irish economy is vulnerable to an oil production peak, as well as the policies required for preparing for such an event. Speaking on the launch of the report, Martin Cronin, Chief Executive of Forfás, commented:

> The high probability that a supply of cheap oil will peak over the next 10 to 15 years, poses a serious challenge for the global economy. As peaking is encountered, liquid fuel prices could increase dramatically and governments, businesses and economies could face significant eco-

nomic and social change. Ireland is more dependent on imported oil for our transport and energy requirements than almost every other European country and it will take up to 10 years to significantly reduce this dependence. It is essential that we now begin to prepare for such a challenge.[2]

The Cuban parliament has passed a measure declaring 2006 to be the year of the Energy Revolution. President Fidel Castro, in a speech delivered November 17, 2005, discussed the goal of reducing all energy use in the country by two-thirds. That nation has already dealt successfully with a dramatic forced reduction in oil consumption, consequent upon the collapse of the USSR in the late 1980s.

In the US, the House of Representatives has asked its Subcommittee on Energy and Air Quality to investigate a motion proposed by Representative Roscoe Bartlett of Maryland, "...that the United States, in collaboration with other international allies, should establish an energy project with the magnitude, creativity, and sense of urgency that was incorporated in the 'Man on the Moon' project to address the inevitable challenges of 'Peak Oil.'"[3] In his State of the Union message on January 31, 2006, President Bush said that the US is "addicted to oil" and must "move beyond a petroleum-based economy"; he then put forward the goal of reducing by three-quarters his country's reliance on oil imports from the Middle East by the year 2025.[4] He has also said that "we have got to wean ourselves off hydrocarbons, oil."[5]

With its enormous geothermal energy resources, Iceland in 2001 officially adopted the goal of making the country oil-free by 2050. This small nation of about 270,000 people has a high per-capita rate of greenhouse gas emissions—despite the fact that about 70 percent of its energy needs, from home heating to electricity for aluminum smelters, are met by abundant geothermal or hydroelectric power. Only Iceland's transport sector is still reliant primarily on oil and gas. The nation's leaders plan to run its cars, buses, trucks, and ships on hydrogen produced from electrolysis of water.[6]

Other countries such as Germany, Japan, Spain, and the Netherlands have made important strides in implementing renewable energy technologies (primarily solar and wind). China and India are also investing heavily in renewables, though their consumption of fossil fuels is also growing.

All of these nations can benefit from the Protocol, which will assist them in attaining goals they have either already proposed, or are practically pursuing.

Nevertheless, it would be unrealistic to assume that national leaders will immediately appreciate the benefits of the Protocol or act automatically to adopt it. In some countries longstanding political interests related to the fossil fuel industry might discourage influential politicians from supporting mandated limits on petroleum imports or exports. Also, doctrinaire free-market economists are likely to argue strongly against government interference with the unfettered flux of supply and demand.

Adoption of the Protocol within any given nation will therefore require initially that just a few policy makers have the courage to champion it and bring it before their parliament or congress. We hope to identify those specific politicians and to assist them in persuading their colleagues. Simultaneously, the mobilization of widespread public support can embolden other leaders to join in the push toward adoption, until finally a majority of legislators has been won over and the Protocol gains official acceptance.

One interesting strategy being used increasingly by grass-roots movements to shape government policy from below is Simultaneous Policy (SP). Many environmental initiatives are perceived to carry an economic cost, and are therefore opposed by affected industries that have considerable political clout. Citizens can agree on specific issues they wish to include in SP, then seek to persuade politicians to sign an SP pledge. Politicians who sign the pledge are agreeing to implement SP alongside other governments when all, or sufficient, other nations have agreed to do so. This creates a no-risk situation for politicians to declare their willingness to help solve global problems, while not doing so increases the risk of losing out in elections. Current simultaneous policy proposals include measures for tackling climate change, fair trade, and third-world debt, water rights, corporate responsibility, abolition of WMD, reduction of conventional arms, and monetary reform. The SP website notes:

> Gallup International's "Voice of the people 2005" survey revealed that almost two-thirds of people worldwide do not feel that their country is ruled by the will of the people. This can be seen everywhere as growing numbers are opting out of using their votes. However, eight out of ten people interviewed still believe that in spite of its limitations, democracy is the best system of government. SP gives the increasingly large portion of non-voting citizens a reason to go back to the polling booths, meaning the SP voting bloc could prove to be critical in deciding the outcome of elections.[7]

The Oil Depletion Protocol would be a natural addition to Simultaneous Policy, and is already being discussed and promoted in that context.

Municipal Efforts

Cities around the world are beginning to assess their vulnerability to Peak Oil and are planning to reduce it. Some examples:

Kinsale, Ireland was the first town to undertake a comprehensive Peak Oil assessment and response scenario, titled "The Kinsale Energy Descent Energy Action Plan." The phrase "energy descent" is taken from Howard Odum's book, *The Prosperous Way Down,* and means "transition from a high fossil fuel-use economy to a more frugal one."[8] The project was initiated by Rob Hopkins and his Practical Sustainability class at Further Education College. The resultant 25-year report with a year-to-year plan of action has since been adopted as policy by the Kinsale town council.[9]

The Mayor of Denver, Colorado, John Hickenlooper, is a former exploration geologist who understands the problem of oil depletion in a way that few other city officials do. In November, 2005 Denver hosted a World Oil Forum, sponsored by the Association for the Study of Peak Oil, at which Mayor Hickenlooper—together with industry experts, political leaders, authors, and others—addressed both global and local issues related to energy scarcity. Among the many topics covered was an "exploration of policy options, especially at the municipal level," for addressing the challenge of Peak Oil. Mayor Hickenlooper's administration has reduced Denver's municipal vehicle fleet by seven percent and has begun purchasing hybrids and vehicles that can be fueled with bio diesel. The Denver International Airport uses alternative fuels for all non-flight vehicles. Denver is changing land-use policy to promote high-density zoning areas in conjunction with a new public transit system. The city also promotes full or partial telecommuting to use less fuel.[10]

During the past two years the town of Willits, California has undertaken an assessment of its vulnerability to the effects of Peak Oil, and has produced a plan for energy transition. Dr. Jason Bradford, formerly of the University of California at Davis, facilitated town meetings on Peak Oil after screening the film "The End of Suburbia." These meetings led to the creation of the Willits Economic Localization (WELL) project and resulted in the formation of ad-hoc groups of WELL members to address the problems of providing sustained sources of food, water, shelter, health and medical services, and energy to the community of Willits. Together with WELL and the Willits Ad-Hoc Energy Group, City Councilman Ron Orenstein has sponsored a report for the city of Willits titled "Recommendations towards Energy Independence for the City of Willits and Surrounding Community." The report describes how the area could, given timely action, deal proactively with the problems of oil and gas depletion, achieving energy independence and emerging as a strong, organized, and self-sufficient community.[11]

Sebastopol, California has appointed a commission to study the problem of Peak Oil and make recommendations. Students at New College of California in nearby Santa Rosa are involved in the "Powerdown Project," which offers assistance to Sebastopol and other regional towns in their efforts along these lines.

The Transportation Committee of the City of Burnaby, British Columbia, Canada has produced an excellent report summarizing the challenge of Peak Oil and offering recommendations.[12]

Other municipal, citizen-led efforts now under way in the US include ones in Tompkins County, New York; the San Francisco Bay Area in California; Boulder, Colorado; Plymouth, New Hampshire; Bloomington, Indiana; and Eugene, Oregon, among many others.

Since so much work along these lines has already been accomplished, localities that wish to address the problem of looming fuel shortages can save themselves considerable time by obtaining and closely studying reports that have been produced by some of the municipalities mentioned above—such as those of Kinsale, Willits, and Burnaby, all archived at the website of the Powerdown Project, www. powerdownproject.org.

In countries that have not yet adopted the Oil Depletion Protocol, municipalities, provinces, and citizen groups could further leverage their Peak Oil preparation efforts by publicly agreeing to reduce their oil consumption by 2.6 percent per year according to the terms of the Protocol. Many cities and some states in the US are already taking this kind of proactive approach with regard to the Kyoto greenhouse emissions accord, implementing the terms of the accord locally even as the nation as a whole delays ratifying it. For example, the state of California and a number of states in the New England region of the US have passed laws that support the Kyoto accord and require reductions in greenhouse gas emissions far beyond those currently mandated by the federal government. This same strategy, applied to the Oil Depletion Protocol, will be most effective if the municipalities, groups, or regions concerned announce publicly that they are abiding by the Protocol and recommend its adoption to national political leaders.

Personal Efforts

Just as municipalities can help enact the Protocol, with the Protocol also helping municipalities meet their own Peakpreparedness goals, individuals and small groups can help as well.

The best way to begin implementing the Protocol at this smallest of levels would be to carefully read the Kinsale and Willits reports, and then think of personal implications and of how these plans could be adapted to the household. Just as a nation or municipality begins with an inventory and a vulnerability assessment, and then creates a year-by-year plan of action, the individual or family can do the same.

First, create an oil inventory. Where and how are you using both petroleum and the products and services derived from it? If you drive a personal automobile, it will be a simple matter to keep track of how many gallons of gasoline you use. Also, keep track of how many miles you fly this year, and assume a fuel usage for those miles approximately equal to your fuel usage while driving. The greater challenge will be in tracking indirect petroleum usage in food, plastics, and chemicals. On average, for a typical urbanite in an industrialized country, nearly half of oil consumed goes toward transportation, one-third toward food provisioning (including agriculture, transportation of product, storage, and processing), and the rest toward the production of plastics and chemicals. This assessment process will be even more helpful if it is part of an overall energy inventory that includes electricity and natural gas; however, for the purpose of your fulfilment of the terms of the Protocol, keep track of other energy usage separately.

Next, think about your vulnerabilities to higher oil costs and to national shortfalls or rationing. Could you still get to work, and to the shopping areas you depend on? How might food prices be affected? In what other ways might your life be impacted? Compile a list and think about it in terms of various scenarios—for example, with oil at 50 percent above its current price, at double its current price, and triple its current price; with gasoline available only in smaller quantities; and with driving permitted only on alternate days.

Finally, begin to formulate responses to address these vulnerabilities. Make a plan, in year-by-year stages, covering at least the next ten years. During those ten years, you must find a way to reduce your consumption of oil by a total of about 25 percent. With some effort, it may be possible to make that entire reduction in the first year, though this need not be your goal. However, in the very first year you should aim to achieve a minimal 2.6 percent reduction (for ease of calculation, you may wish to round up these percentages to three percent per year.

For both individuals and nations, transportation is the area of greatest dependence and vulnerability with regard to petroleum. It is also the area in which it is easiest to make measurable reductions in oil usage. Reduce driving, and make your travel more efficient by trading an existing car for a smaller and more fuel-efficient model. Or, better yet, find a way to do without a car. Ride a bicycle or electric scooter. Take public transportation where it is available, and, where it isn't, help organize other options, such as a car co-op or a community-supported hitchhiking program. Reduce your air travel to a minimum.

Reduce oil dependence with regard to your eating habits by buying local, organic food. Shop at farmers' markets or join a community-supported agriculture program. And if you live where this is possible, grow a vegetable garden and plant fruit and nut trees. Keep track of what percentage of your food is organically grown and what percentage is grown within 100 miles of where you live. Making a shift from conventionally grown and imported food to food that is 100 percent organically grown and 50 percent locally grown might account for up to five years' worth of personal oil dependency reduction under terms of the Protocol (at three percent per year).

Avoid using plastic wherever possible, especially in the form of packaging. Carry reusable cloth bags with you when you go shopping, and do not buy water in throw-away plastic bottles. If you do these things consistently, you can credit yourself with a two-percent reduction in oil dependence.

These efforts will be of much greater value if they are undertaken in the context of a well-publicized, cooperative local program:

- Tell your friends and family what you are doing and why. Explain to them the problem of Peak Oil and the benefits offered by the Oil Depletion Protocol, and let them know how your personal efforts are contributing to the latter.
- Form a support network within your community and hold periodic public events to promote oil-free behaviors. Make the experience fun for people of all ages by including music, public artwork, and dance. The organization City Repair in Portland, Oregon has been helping facilitate similar events for several years.[13]
- Inform your local officials about Peak Oil and about the Oil Depletion Protocol through letters, and request meetings in order to explain further.
- Work with your community officials to establish a commission to assess community vulnerability and to design a transition plan.

- Seek to obtain endorsement of the Oil Depletion Protocol from your municipality, and from organizations of which you are a member.
- Document your efforts and post periodic summaries to www.oildepletionprotocol.org.

Finally, please help spread the word about the Oil Depletion Protocol by lending this book to family, friends, colleagues, and local officials, and by purchasing a copy for your local library.

The next few years may offer humankind a last, best opportunity to avert resource wars, terrorism, and economic collapse as we enter the second half of the Age of Oil. But more, if we grasp that opportunity and succeed, we could set a precedent for cooperative, peaceful approaches to all of the resource problems and conflicts we are likely to encounter during the coming century.

The choice we face is between competition and conflict on one hand, and voluntary moderation and mutual assistance on the other. If we do nothing, the former will be our default choice. The latter will require enormous effort, but the stakes are very high and even partial success may make all the difference in the world.

APPENDIX 1:

THE OIL DEPLETION

PROTOCOL

As drafted by Dr. Colin J. Campbell*

WHEREAS the passage of history has recorded an increasing pace of change, such that the demand for energy has grown rapidly in parallel with the world population over the past two hundred years since the Industrial Revolution;

WHEREAS the energy supply required by the population has come mainly from coal and petroleum, such resources having been formed but rarely in the geological past and being inevitably subject to depletion;

WHEREAS oil provides ninety percent of transport fuel, is essential to trade, and plays a critical role in the agriculture needed to feed the expanding population;

WHEREAS oil is unevenly distributed on the Planet for well-understood geological reasons, with much being concentrated in five countries bordering the Persian Gulf;

---

*This text, with slight changes in wording, has elsewhere been published as "The Rimini Protocol" and "The Uppsala Protocol."

WHEREAS all the major productive provinces of the World have been identified with the help of advanced technology and growing geological knowledge, it being now evident that discovery reached a peak in the 1960s, despite technological progress and a diligent search;

WHEREAS the past peak of discovery inevitably leads to a corresponding peak in production during the first decade of the 21st Century, assuming no radical decline in demand;

WHEREAS the onset of the decline of this critical resource affects all aspects of modern life, such having grave political and geopolitical implications;

WHEREAS it is expedient to plan an orderly transition to the new World environment of reduced energy supply, making early provisions to avoid the waste of energy, stimulate the entry of substitute energies, and extend the life of the remaining oil;

WHEREAS it is desirable to meet the challenges so arising in a co-operative and equitable manner, such to address related climate change concerns, economic and financial stability, and the threats of conflicts for access to critical resources.

NOW IT IS PROPOSED THAT
1. A convention of nations shall be called to consider the issue with a view to agreeing an Accord with the following objectives:
   a. to avoid profiteering from shortage, such that oil prices may remain in reasonable relationship with production cost;
   b. to allow poor countries to afford their imports;

   c. to avoid destabilizing financial flows arising from excessive oil prices;

   d. to encourage consumers to avoid waste;

   e. to stimulate the development of alternative energies.

2. Such an Accord shall have the following outline provisions:

   a. The world and every nation shall aim to reduce oil consumption by at least the world depletion rate.

   b. No country shall produce oil at above its present depletion rate.

   c. No country shall import at above the world depletion rate.

   d. The depletion rate is defined as annual production as a percent of what is left (reserves plus yet-to-find).

   e. The preceding provisions refer to regular conventional oil—which category excludes heavy oils with cut-off of 17.5 API, deepwater oil with a cut-off of 500 meters, polar oil, gas liquids from gas fields, tar sands, oil shale, oil from coal, biofuels such as ethanol, etc.

3. Detailed provisions shall cover the definition of the several categories of oil, exemptions and qualifications, and the scientific procedures for the estimation of Depletion Rate.

4. The signatory countries shall cooperate in providing information on their reserves, allowing full technical audit, such that the Depletion Rate may be accurately determined.

5. The signatory countries shall have the right to appeal their assessed Depletion Rate in the event of changed circumstances.

APPENDIX 2:

SOURCES OF FURTHER

INFORMATION

On Oil Depletion:
www.globalpublicmedia.com
www.encrgybulletin.net
www.peakoil.net
www.theoildrum.com
www.odac-info.org

On Domestic Tradable Quotas (TEQs):
www.TEQs.org

On the Hirsch Report:
www.cge.uevora.pt/aspo2005/abscom/Abstract_Lisbon_
  Hirsch.pdf
www.hilltoplancers.org/stories/hirscho502.pdf

On Local Efforts
www.postcarbon.org
Darley, Julian, David Room, Richard Heinberg and Celine
  Rich. *Relocalize Now! Getting Ready for Climate Change
  and the End of Cheap Oil.* New Society, 2006. (In press)

APPENDIX 3
WORLD REGULAR CONVENTIONAL OIL PRODUCTION TO 2100

		PRESENT		PAST		REPORTED RESERVES		DEDUCTIONS			FUTURE	
COUNTRY	REGION CODES	KB/D 2004	GB/A 2004	TOTAL	5 YR TREND (%)	WORLD OIL	O&GJ	STATIC	OTHER	% REPT'D	FUTURE	TOTAL
Saudi Arabia	A	8750	3.19	100	2	259	259	-40	0	160	162	263
Russia	B	8950	3.27	130	8	65	60	-6	-37	80	75	205
US-48	C	3560	1.30	173	-4	23	22	0	-9	90	24	198
Iran	A	3940	1.44	57	1	105	126	-21	0	180	70	127
Iraq	A	2070	0.76	29	-4	115	115	-9	0	185	62	91
Kuwait	A	2050	0.75	32	3	97	99	0	0	180	55	87
Venezuela	D	1879	0.69	47	-5	52	77	0	-30	225	34	82
Abu Dhabi	A	1955	0.71	19	1	65	92	-11	0	230	40	59
China	B	3494	1.28	31	2	16	18	-2.5	0	75	24	55
Mexico	D	3410	1.24	32	3	15	15	0.0	0	70	21	53
Libya	E	1550	0.57	24	2	31	39	0.0	0	190	21	44
Nigeria	E	2350	0.86	24	3	33	35	0.0	-6	175	20	44
Kazakhstan	B	986	0.36	7	9	-	9.0	-0.7	0	30	30	37
Norway	F	2940	1.07	19	-2	9.4	8.5	0.0	0	75	11	30
UK	F	1830	0.67	21	-5	4.3	4.5	0.0	0	60	7.5	29
Indonesia	G	973	0.36	21	-5	5.5	4.7	-0.4	0	60	7.8	28
Algeria	E	1205	0.41	13	10	14.0	11.8	0.0	0	95	12	25
Canada	C	1100	0.01	20	0	5.0	179	-0.4	-175	3100	5.8	25
Azerbaijan	B	298	0.11	8.3	2	-	7.0	-0.2	0	60	12	20
N.Zone	A	597	0.22	7.1	-1	4.75	5.0	-2.4	0	95	5.3	12.3
Argentina	D	680	0.26	8.5	-2	2.7	2.7	0.0	0	75	3.6	12.1
Oman	H	767	0.28	7.6	-18	5.7	5.5	-1.3	0	110	5.0	12.6
Egypt	E	712	0.26	9.2	-2	2.3	3.7	0.0	0	120	3.1	12.3
India	G	685	0.25	6.1	1	4.0	5.4	-0.3	0	120	4.5	10.6
Qatar	H	782	0.29	7.3	3	27.4	15.2	-0.8	-25	375	4.1	11.4
Malaysia	G	855	0.31	5.9	5	3.1	3.0	-0.9	0	75	4.0	9.9
Colombia	D	530	0.20	5.9	-5	1.5	1.5	-0.4	0	50	3.1	9.0
Australia	G	430	0.16	6.1	-8	4.0	1.5	0.0	-1	80	1.9	8.0
Angola	E	480	0.18	5.0	-7	8.9	5.4	-2.0	-10	140	3.9	8.8
Ecuador	D	518	0.19	3.6	6	5.0	4.6	-0.3	0	110	4.2	7.8
Brasil	D	400	0.15	4.97	2	9.8	8.5	0.0	-12	425	2.00	7.0
Romania	B	102	0.04	5.83	-3	0.5	1.0	-0.1	0	110	0.87	6.7
Syria	H	504	0.18	4.17	-1	2.4	2.5	-2.2	0	100	2.50	6.7
Turkmenistan	B	216	0.08	3.10	10	-	0.55	-0.3	0	50	1.09	4.2
Dubai	H	350	0.13	3.99	5	1.23	4.00	-2.2	0	500	0.80	4.8

Note: Gb (billion barrels)

COUNTRY	NEW FIELDS	ALL FUTURE	TOTAL	DEPLETION		PEAK	
				RATE	MIDPOINT	DISC	PROD
Saudi Arabia	12.4	175	275	1.80	2015	1948	2013
Russia	14.6	90	220	3.5	1996	1960	1987
US-48	2.3	27	200	4.6	1971	1930	1971
Iran	12.9	83	140	1.71	2013	1961	1974
Iraq	9.2	71	100	1.05	2025	1928	2025
Kuwait	2.7	58	90	1.28	2020	1938	2015
Venezuela	5.7	40	88	3.2	1999	1941	1970
Abu Dhabi	5.5	46	65	1.54	2021	1964	2021
China	4.6	29	60	4.2	2003	1959	2003
Mexico	2.7	24	56	5.0	2000	1977	2004
Libya	5.5	26	50	2.1	2005	1961	1970
Nigeria	3.8	24	48	3.1	2004	1967	2004
Kazakhstan	8.3	38	45	0.9	2036	2000	2030
Norway	3.2	14.5	33	6.9	2002	1979	2001
UK	2.4	9.9	31	6.3	1997	1974	1999
Indonesia	1.6	9.4	30	3.62	1992	1945	1977
Algeria	2.6	15.0	28	2.8	2006	1956	1978
Canada	0.7	6.4	26	5.9	1987	1958	1973
Azerbaijan	2.5	14.2	23	0.8	2014	1871	2009
N.Zone	1.7	6.9	14	3.0	2004	1951	2003
Argentina	0.9	4.5	13	5.5	1996	1960	1998
Oman	0.4	5.4	13	4.9	2001	1962	2001
Egypt	0.7	3.8	13	6.4	1995	1965	1995
India	0.9	5.4	12	4.4	2003	1974	2004
Qatar	0.1	4.2	12	6.4	1998	1940	2004
Malaysia	0.6	4.6	11	6.4	2002	1973	2004
Colombia	1.0	4.1	10	4.8	1999	1992	1999
Australia	2.0	3.9	10	3.9	1999	1967	2000
Angola	0.7	4.5	10	3.7	2004	1971	1998
Ecuador	0.2	4.4	8.0	4.1	2006	1969	2004
Brasil	0.0	2.0	7.0	6.7	1995	1975	1986
Romania	0.3	1.17	7.0	3.1	1970	1857	1976
Syria	0.3	2.83	7.0	6.1	2000	1966	1995
Turkmenistan	1.3	2.40	5.5	3.2	1998	1964	1973
Dubai	0.2	1.01	5.0	11.3	1991	1970	1991

World Regular Conventional Oil Production To 2100 (continued)

KNOWN FIELDS

		PRESENT		PAST							FUTURE	
						REPORTED RESERVES						
COUNTRY	REGION CODES	KB/D 2004	GB/A 2004	TOTAL	5 YR TREND (%)	WORLD OIL	O&GJ	DEDUCTIONS STATIC	OTHER	% REPT'D	FUTURE	TOTAL
Trinidad	D	130	0.05	3.30	2	0.76	0.99	-0.1	0	85	1.16	4.5
Brunei	G	190	0.07	3.14	1	1.05	1.35	-0.9	0	110	1.23	4.4
Gabon	E	235	0.09	3.02	-6	2.29	2.50	-0.7	0	170	1.47	4.5
Ukraine	B	80	0.03	2.72	2	-	0.40	-0.1	0	40	0.99	3.7
Denmark	F	393	0.14	1.61	5	1.28	1.32	0.0	0	120	1.32	2.9
Yemen	H	350	0.13	1.87	0	2.85	4.00	-1.5	0	340	1.18	3.0
Peru	D	81	0.03	2.39	-3	0.90	0.95	0.0	-1	110	0.87	3.3
Vietnam	G	340	0.12	1.14	2	2.28	0.60	-0.8	0	30	2.00	3.1
Uzbekistan	B	134	0.05	1.16	-3	-	0.59	-0.3	0	50	1.19	2.3
Congo	E	240	0.09	1.69	-2	1.43	1.51	-0.9	-1	210	0.72	2.4
Germany	F	69	0.03	1.98	2	0.26	0.39	0.0	0	120	0.33	2.3
Italy	F	115	0.04	0.96	5	0.49	0.62	-0.1	-0.3	80	0.78	1.7
Sudan	E	287	0.10	0.44	11	6.31	0.56	-0.3	0	50	1.13	1.56
Tunisia	E	70	0.03	1.25	-2	0.50	0.31	-0.2	0	75	0.41	1.66
Chad	E	247	0.09	0.13	-	-	-	0.0	0	-	1.20	1.33
Thailand	G	154	0.06	0.54	8	0.50	0.58	-0.1	0	80	0.73	1.27
Cameroon	E	70	0.02	1.08	-5	-	0.40	-0.7	0	110	0.36	1.44
Bolivia	D	35	0.01	0.45	5	0.46	0.44	0.0	0	80	0.55	1.00
Bahrain	H	34	0.01	1.00	2	-	0.12	0.0	0	60	0.21	1.21
Netherlands	F	44	0.02	0.86	10	0.05	0.11	0.0	0	40	0.27	1.12
Turkey	H	42	0.02	0.86	-5	0.26	0.30	0.0	0	150	0.20	1.06
Croatia	B	19	0.01	0.51	-3	0.06	0.08	0.0	0	24	0.31	0.82
Hungary	B	22	0.01	0.69	-5	0.14	0.10	0.0	0	70	0.15	0.84
France	F	23	0.01	0.74	-4	0.15	0.15	0.0	0	95	0.15	0.90
Pakistan	G	62	0.02	0.50	15	0.29	0.29	0.0	0	100	0.29	0.79
Austria	F	18	0.01	0.79	-1	0.08	0.06	0.0	0	70	0.09	0.88
Papua	G	46	0.02	0.38	-8	0.31	0.24	0.0	0	70	0.34	0.72
Sharjah	H	48	0.02	0.50	-1	-	1.50	0.0	0	1000	0.15	0.65
Albania	B	6	0.00	0.54	1	0.20	0.17	0.0	0	85	0.19	0.73
Chile	D	10	0.00	0.43	9	0.08	0.15	0.0	0	400	0.04	0.47
REGIONS												
ME Gulf	A	19362	7.07	245	1	641	696	-82	0	177	395	640
Eurasia	B	14308	5.22	191	6	82	97	-11	-37	67	146	337
N. America	C	4660	1.70	193	-2	28	201	0	-184	667	30	223
L. America	D	7673	2.80	110	-1	88	112	-1	-43	158	71	181
Africa	E	7438	2.71	83	2	101	100	-5	-16	154	65	148
Europe	F	5431	1.98	47	0	16	16	0	0	72	22	68
East	G	3735	1.36	44	-1	21	18	-3	-1	77	23	67
ME. Other	H	2877	1.05	27	0	40	33	-8	-25	235	14	41
Other		647	0.24	4	7	-	0	0	0	93	1	5
Unforeseen											6	
Non-M East		46769	16.8	682	1	375	577	-29	-305	155	372	1053
WORLD		66131	24.1	944	1	1016	1273	-111	-305	164	777	1721

COUNTRY	NEW FIELDS	ALL FUTURE	TOTAL	DEPLETION		PEAK	
				RATE	MIDPOINT	DISC	PROD
Trinidad	0.3	1.45	4.8	3.2	1985	1959	1978
Brunei	0.1	1.36	4.5	4.8	1989	1929	1978
Gabon	0.0	1.48	4.5	5.5	1997	1985	1996
Ukraine	0.3	1.28	4.0	2.2	1984	1962	1970
Denmark	0.6	1.89	3.5	7.1	2005	1971	2004
Yemen	0.5	1.63	3.5	7.3	2003	1978	1999
Peru	0.2	1.11	3.5	2.7	1988	1861	1983
Vietnam	0.4	2.36	3.5	5.0	2009	1975	2005
Uzbekistan	0.4	1.59	2.8	3.0	2008	1992	1998
Congo	0.3	1.06	2.8	7.7	2000	1984	2001
Germany	0.2	0.52	2.5	4.6	1977	1952	1966
Italy	0.3	1.0	2.0	3.9	2005	1981	2004
Sudan	0.6	1.76	2.2	5.6	2009	1980	2005
Tunisia	0.3	0.75	2.0	3.3	1998	1971	1981
Chad	0.7	1.87	2.0	4.6	2014	1977	2008
Thailand	0.3	1.06	1.60	5.0	2008	1981	2005
Cameroon	0.1	0.42	1.50	5.1	1994	1977	1986
Bolivia	0.3	0.80	1.25	1.6	2016	1966	2010
Bahrain	0.0	0.25	1.25	5.0	1977	1932	1970
Netherlands	0.1	0.34	1.20	4.5	1991	1980	1989
Turkey	0.1	0.34	1.20	4.3	1992	1969	1991
Croatia	0.2	0.49	1.00	1.4	2003	1950	1988
Hungary	0.2	0.31	1.00	2.6	1987	1964	1987
France	0.1	0.21	0.95	3.9	1987	1958	1988
Pakistan	0.4	0.40	0.90	5.4	2001	1983	1992
Austria	0.0	0.11	0.90	5.6	1970	1947	1955
Papua	0.1	0.47	0.85	3.4	2007	1987	1993
Sharjah	0.1	0.30	0.80	5.6	1998	1980	1998
Albania	0.1	0.26	0.80	0.9	1986	1928	1983
Chile	0.0	0.07	0.50	4.8	1979	1960	1982
REGIONS							
ME Gulf	44	439	684	1.58	2017	1948	1974
Eurasia	33	179	370	2.8	2003	1964	1987
N. America	3	33	226	4.9	1973	1930	1972
L. America	11	82	192	3.3	1999	1977	1998
Africa	15	81	163	3.0	2004	1961	2004
Europe	7	29	75	6.5	2000	1974	2000
East	6	29	73	4.5	1999	1967	2000
ME. Other	2	16	43	6.2	1999	1965	1998
Other	5	6	10	3.7	2009	1956	2007
Unforeseen	7	13	13				
Non-M East	103	474	1156	3.4	1996	1956	2004
WORLD	129	906	1850	2.6	2004	1964	2004

NOTES

Chapter 1: The Challenge of Peak Oil

1. Natural gas shortages may occur in North America and some other regions concurrently with oil shortages.
2. While volumes of oil are often measured in barrels for historic reasons, very little oil these days ever sees the inside of a barrel. Oil is also measured in tons; one ton of crude oil equals approximately 7.3 barrels of crude oil (assuming a specific gravity of 33 API). See www.eppo .go.th/ref/UNIT-OIL.html.
3. Available supply refers to oil actually extracted or produced and thus delivered to the market, not to oil theoretically existing in reserves.
4. This could be thought of as a plateau period of gyrating prices, with both political and economic events, and natural disasters as likely triggers.
5. This figure is, of course, a matter of conjecture. Declines in rates of production from some post-peak oilfields are sometimes as high as 10 percent per year or even more; however, given ongoing development of new production projects, including deepwater, polar, natural gas liquids and condensates, heavy oil, and oil sands, this figure (two percent per year) seems reasonable. See ASPO projections updated in the monthly ASPO newsletter, e.g.,

www.peakoil.ie/downloads/newsletters/newsletter64_
200604.pdf [Cited April 6, 2006].

6. Jesse Ausubel and Cesare Marchetti. "The Evolution of Transport" [online]. [Cited April 12, 2006]. *The Industrial Physicist,* April-May 2001. www.tipmagazine.com/tip/INPHFA/vol-7/iss-2/p20.pdf.

7. Norman E. Borlaug. "Feeding a World of 10 Billion People: The Miracle Ahead" [online]. [Cited April 12, 2006]. www.ars.usda.gov/is/kids/globalscitech/borlaug.htm.

8. G. Tyler Miller, Jr. *Living in the Environment,* 11th ed. Brooks/Cole, 2000.

9. Daniel Smith. "Worldwide trends in DDT levels in human breast milk." *International Journal of Epidemiology* 28 (1999): 179–188.

10. Miller, *op. cit.,* pp. 443, 537.

11. John Peterson Myers. "Our Stolen Future: Background on BPA..." [online]. [Cited January 17, 2006]. Our Stolen Future. www.ourstolenfuture.org/NewScience/oncompounds/bisphenola/bpauses.htm.

12. Miller, *op. cit.,* p. 501.

13. "Global Warming: New Scenarios from the Intergovernmental Panel on Climate Change." *Population and Development Review,* 27 no. 1 (2001): 203–208.

14. World Health Organization. "Climate Change and Human Health." *Population and Development Review,* 23 no. 1 (1997): 205–208.

15. Richard Black. "CO_2 'highest for 650,000 years'" [online]. [Cited January 17, 2006]. *BBC News Online.* http://news.bbc.co.uk/1/hi/sci/tech/4467420.stm.

16. "Major Greenland Glacier, Once Stable, Now Shrinking Dramatically" [online]. [Cited January 17, 2006]. *Science Daily.* www.sciencedaily.com/releases/2003/12/031208140730.htm.

17. "Blair moves to end growing UK fuel crisis" [online]. [Cited January 17, 2006]. *CNN*, September 12, 2000. http://edition.cnn.com/2000/WORLD/europe/09/12/ london.fuel.02.

18. See the Chevron website at www.willyoujoinus.com/ issues/alternatives/. [Cited April 12, 2006].

19. Colin Campbell. "ExxonMobil accepts Peak Oil" [online]. [Cited April 6, 2006]. www.peakoil.ie/newsletters/ 577.

20. Bubba. "2005 Exploration Round-Up" [online]. [Cited March 4, 2006]. www.theoildrum.com/story/2006/2/ 28/21235/1491#more.

21. "Statements on Oil" [online]. [Cited October 17, 2005]. Royal Swedish Academy of Sciences Energy Committee, October 17, 2005. www.energybulletin.net/9824.html.

22. For longer discussions of these points see: http://pubs .usgs.gov/dds/dds-060/, www.hubbertpeak.com/ duncan/usgs2000.htm. Evidently, other branches of the US government harbor doubts about the conclusions or methodology of the USGS study: a US Army Corps of Engineers report released in 2005 notes, "The supply of oil will remain fairly stable in the very near term, but oil prices will steadily increase as world production ap- proaches its peak. The doubling of oil prices in the past couple of years is not an anomaly, but a picture of the future. Peak oil is at hand. . . ." See Adam Fenderson and Bart Anderson. "US Army: Peak Oil and the Army's Future" [online]. [Cited March 13, 2006]. *Energy Bul- letin*, March 13, 2006. www.energybulletin.net/13737 .html.

23. Klaus Rehaag. "Is the World Facing a 3rd Oil Shock?" [online]. [Cited April 6, 2006]. July 2004. www.iea.org //textbase/speech/2004/kr_rio.pdf.

24. The CERA study is not available to the public, but their press release "Oil & Liquids Capacity to Outstrip Demand Until At Least 2010: New CERA Report June 21, 2005" is at www.cera.com/news/details/1,2318,7453, 00.html.

25. Chris Skrebowski. "Prices set firm, despite massive new capacity" [online]. Petroleum Review, November 2005. www.globalpublicmedia.com/articles/539.

26. Stuart Staniford. "Exxon, and the Implications of 8%" [online]. [Cited January 22, 2006]. The Oil Drum: A Community Discussion About Peak Oil, November 17, 2005. www.theoildrum.com/story/2005/11/16/182053/32.

27. Ibid.

28. John Gowdy and Roxana Juliá. "Technology and Petroleum Exhaustion: Evidence from Two Mega-Oilfields" [online]. [Cited January 22, 2006]. *Rensselaer Working Papers in Economics,* 512. www.rpi.edu/dept/economics/ www/workingpapers/rpi0512.pdf.

29. During the early 1980s, OPEC decided to link production quotas to stated reserves; this seems to have provided an incentive for member countries to overstate reserves. Reserves estimates of nearly all OPEC countries were increased substantially during that decade, while few major discoveries were reported. Some analysts believe that OPEC reserves are thus overstated by a total of up to 300 billion barrels.

30. SEC rules permit the reporting of reserves only from fields, or portions of fields, in active production. Thus as oilfields are drilled out over the course of many years, companies operating them report reserve increases. Reserve increases are reported for fields discovered decades ago.

31. Recently the US Energy Information Administration has begun including Canadian tar sands under the category of "proven reserves" of oil. However, the production of oil from the tar sands is a very different process from the extraction of regular oil, and entails the use of large quantities of natural gas and fresh water. Thus the rate of extraction is constrained by the availability of these resources, among other factors.

32. "Internationl Energy Outlook 2005" [online]. [Cited April 15, 2006]. Report #DOE/EIA 0484 (2005). www.eia.doe.gov/oiaf/ieo/pdf/ieoreftab_4.pdf.

33. James Schlesinger. Statement before the Committee on Foreign Relations, United States Senate, November 16, 2005 [online]. [Cited March 13, 2006]. www.senate.gov/~foreign/testimony/2005/SchlesingerTestimony051116.pdf.

34. Adam Porter. "Peak Oil enters Mainstream Debate." [online]. [Cited April 6, 2006]. *BBC*, June 10, 2005. http://news.bbc.co.uk/1/hi/business/4077802.stm.

35. Anne Stevens. "Ford Exec: Oil Production is Peaking" [online]. [Cited March 13, 2006]. October 16, 2005. www.greencarcongress.com/2005/10/ford_exec_oil_p.html.

36. "Future fuels for Commercial Vehicles" [online]. [Cited March 13, 2006]. www.volvo.com/NR/rdonlyres/A9A59F6A-AA6F-F48E-A048-BF9D6DE505DB/0/future_fuels_large.pdf.

37. Michael DesLauriers. "Famed Oil Tycoon Sounds Off on Peak Oil" [online]. [Cited March 13, 2006]. *Resource Investor,* June 23, 2005. www.resourceinvestor.com/pebble.asp?relid=10766.

38. Jeroen Van Der Veer. "Vision for Meeting Energy Needs

Beyond Oil" [online]. [Cited March 13, 2006]. *Financial Times,* January 24, 2006. http://news.ft.com/cms/s/fb7 75ee8-8d0e-11da-9daf-0000779e2340.html.

39. "Global Energy Markets: Worse than You May Think" [online]. [Cited March 13, 2006]. Lunch discussion with J. Robinson West, the Nixon Center, June 28, 2005. http://72.14.203.104/search?q=cache:G5QeooUa _IsJ:www.nixoncenter.org/Program%2520Briefs/PB20 05/Vol11no12GlobalEnergyMarkets.pdf.

40. Michael DesLauriers. "Oil Forecasting Legend Discusses Peak Oil, Share Prices" [online]. [Cited March 13, 2006]. *Resource Investor,* October 19, 2005. www.resource investor.com/pebble.asp?relid=13837.

41. Robert B. Semple, Jr. "The End of Oil" [online]. [Cited March 13, 2006]. *New York Times,* March 1, 2006. http:// select.nytimes.com/gst/tsc.html?URI=http://select.ny times.com/2006/03/01/opinion/01talkingpoints.html& OQ=_rQ3D1Q26pagewantedQ3Dall&OP=65dfb2d 8Q2F)GQ24E)DQ5CH00D)Q22rrI)ri)rK)oLQ2AQ 7EQ2AoQ7E)rKDQ26.Q7BQ2AQ7EgLoQ2AQ7ED Q5CxkD2.

42. Kenneth Deffeyes. "Current Events: Join us as we watch the crisis unfolding" [online]. [Cited February 18, 2006]. *Beyond Oil,* February 11, 2006. www.princeton.edu/ hubbert/current-events.html.

43. "Henry Groppe Talks about Peak Oil During ASPO USA Conference" [online]. Global Public Media, November 11, 2005. www.globalpublicmedia.com/ interviews/597.

44. Ali Samsam Bakhtiari. "World Oil Production Capacity Model Suggests Output Peak by 2006–07." *Oil and Gas*

Journal, April 26, 2004. www.energybulletin.net/147
.html.

45. Richard Duncan. "Heuristic Oil Forecasting Method
    #4 Forecasting Paper" [online]. [Cited February 18,
    2006]. June 17, 2001. www.mnforsustain.org/oil_
    duncan_r_heuristic_oil_forecasting_paper.htm.

46. ODAC. "Oil field mega projects" [online]. [Cited
    February 18, 2006]. *E&P Review* (2004). www.odac-
    info.org/bulletin/documents/MEGAPROJECTS
    REPORT.pdf.

47. Colin Campbell. "Peak Oil: an Outlook on Crude Oil
    Depletion" [online]. [Cited February 18, 2006].
    www.greatchange.org/ov-campbell,outlook.html.

48. Rembrandt Koppelaar. "Oil Production Outlook 2005–
    2040" [online]. [Coted February 18, 2006]. Foundation
    Peak Oil Netherlands, September 6, 2005. http://sydney
    peakoil.com/downloads/oil_production_outlook_
    2005-2040.pdf.

49. Jean Laherrere. "Hydrocarbons Resources Forecast of
    oil and gas supply to 2050" [online]. [Cited February 18,
    2006]. Petrotech conference, New Delhi, 2003. www
    .hubbertpeak.com/laherrere/Petrotech090103.pdf.

50. PFC Energy. "Energy Insecurity" [online] [Cited Febru-
    ary 18, 2006]. Testimony of J. Robinson West Chairman
    PFC Energy, September 21, 2005. http://commerce.
    senate.gov/pdf/west.pdf.

51. CERA. "Worldwide Liquids Capacity Outlook to 2010:
    Tight Supply or Excess of Riches?" [online]. [Cited
    February 18, 2006]. 2005. www.cera.com/attachment/
    view/0,2017,23649,00.pdf.

52. USGS. "Long-Term World Oil Supply: A Resource

Base/Production Path Analysis" [online]. [Cited February 18, 2006]. Energy Information Administration, US Department of Energy. www.eia.doe.gov/emeu/plugs/plworld.html.

53. Robert L. Hirsch, Roger Bezdek, and Robert Wendling. "Peaking of World Oil Production: Impacts, Mitigation, and Risk Management" [online]. [Cited February 18, 2006]. SAIC, February 2005. www.netl.doe.gov/publications/others/pdf/Oil_Peaking_NETL.pdf.

54. "The Early Days of Coal Research: Wartime Needs Spur Interest in Coal-to-Oil Processes" [online]. [Cited January 22, 2006]. United States Department of Energy, January 10, 2006. www.fe.doe.gov/aboutus/history/syntheticfuels_history.html.

55. Ken Silverstein. "Coal Liquefaction Plants Spark Hope" [online]. [Cited January 22, 2006]. UtiliPoint International, Inc., November 1, 2004. www.utilipoint.com/issuealert/article.asp?id=2314.

56. "Carbon Sequestration" [online]. [Cited February 18, 2006]. US Department of Energy, November 6, 2005. www.fossil.energy.gov/programs/sequestration/.

57. Hirsch, *op. cit.*, p. 43.

58. Chandra B. Prakash, PhD. "A Critical Review of Biodiesel as a Transportation Fuel in Canada" [online]. [Cited January 22, 2006]. Global Change Strategies International Inc. for Environment Canada, Air Pollution Prevention Directorate. www.a1biofuel.com/files/Biodeisel%20transportation%20fuel%20in%20canada%20report.pdf.

59. Biodiesel density (average) = 0.88 kg/liter. 1 (metric) ton = 1000 kg and 158.984 liters = 1 barrel, so 1 barrel =

0.139906 ton biodiesel. 3 million tons biodiesel =
approx. 21 million barrels.

60. "Industry Argues That Ethanol Delivers" [online].
[Cited January 22, 2006]. *Rooster News Network*, September 4, 2001. http://journeytoforever.org/ethanol
_rooster.html.

61. "Energy Equivalents of Various Fuels" [online]. [Cited
February 28, 2006]. National Association of Fleet
Administrators, Inc., 2002. www.nafa.org/Content/
NavigationMenu/Resource_Center/Alternative_
Fuels/Energy_Equivalents/Energy_Equivalents.htm.

62. David Granatstein. "Renewable Fuels for PHEVs" [online]. [Cited February 18, 2006]. Center for Sustaining
Agriculture and Natural Resources, November 2005.
www.ncwctc.com/files/documents/4_David_G_-_Bio
fuels.pdf.

63. G. Berndes, M.M. Hoogwijk, and R. van den Broek.
"The contribution of biomass in the future global energy
system: a review of 17 studies." *Biomass & Bioenergy*, 25,
no. 1 (2003): 1–28.

64. Ted Trainer. "Chapter 5: Liquid and Gaseous Fuels Derived from Biomass" [online]. [Cited January 22, 2006].
Renewable Energy: Limits and Potential. University of
New South Wales, April 2004. http://socialwork.arts
.unsw.edu.au/tsw/D86.RE.Ch.5.LiquidsX.html. Entire
manuscript: http://socialwork.arts.unsw.edu
.au/tsw/D74.RENEWABLE-ENERGY.html.

65. The idea of a "hydrogen economy" is discussed in somewhat more detail in Chapter 4.

66. From www.eia.doe.gov/oiaf/aeo/supplement/suptab_
49.xls [Cited April 6, 2006]. Which is a table from the

Supplemental Tables (www.eia.doe.gov/oiaf/aeo/sup-
plement/) to the EIA's "Annual Energy Outlook 2006
with Projections to 2030" (www.eia.doe.gov/oiaf/
aeo). Average New Car On-Road MPG (by year) =
2003: 22.069; 2004: 22.274; 2005: 22.448; 2006:
22.543.

Chapter 2: Without the Protocol

1. Unlike other oil-importing industrial nations, Japan
fared relatively well during this time, as that nation's
automakers designed and produced increasingly popular
small, energy-efficient vehicles. Japan's cities, moreover,
had relatively high population densities and excellent
public transportation infrastructure. In response to the
1973 oil crisis, much of the Japanese economy began to
shift away from oil-intensive heavy industrial production
and toward the manufacturing of electronics.
2. Javier Blas. "IMF Warns High Prices Risk Global Crisis"
[online]. [Cited April 9, 2006]. *Financial Times,* April 6,
2006. https://registration.ft.com/registration/barrier?ref
erer=&location=http%3A//news.ft.com/cms/s/8d37b6
40-c59d-11da-b675-0000779e2340.html.
3. Hirsch, *op. cit,* p. 28.
4. Hirsch, *op. cit,* p. 61.
5. Karim Jaufeerally. "An Elementary Model to Assess the
Impact of Different Levels of Oil Prices on the Mauritian
Economy" [online]. [Cited January 27, 2006]. Institute
for Environmental and Legal Studies, November 2005.
www.intnet.mu/iels/imfl_egs.htm.
6. James Stevenson. "CIBC Report Predicts Oil to Tip
$100 Within 2 Years" [online]. [Cited February 12,

2006]. *Resource Investor*, September 8, 2005.
www.resourceinvestor.com/pebble.asp?relid=12735.

7. Congressional Budget Office. "Energy Use in Freight
Transportation" [online]. [Cited March 4, 2006].
www.cbo.gov/showdoc.cfm?index=5330&sequence=0.

8. "Travel to Work Characteristics for the 50 Largest
Metropolitan Areas by Population in the United States:
1990 Census" [online]. [Cited January 27, 2006]. United
States Census Bureau. www.census.gov/population/soc
demo/journey/msa50.txt; "2000 Census: US Municipalities Over 50,000: Ranked by 2000 Population."
[online]. [Cited January 27, 2006]. Demographia.
www.demographia.com/db-uscity98.htm.

9. "US Public Transport Ridership by Metropolitan Area
Population Classification" [online]. [Cited January 27,
2006]. Urban Transport Fact Book. www.publicpurpose
.com/ut-ride2000class.htm.

10. Elizabeth Roberto. "Commuting Expenses: Disparity
for the Working Poor" [online]. [Cited January 27,
2006]. BTS Issue Brief No. 1, United States Department
of Transportation, Bureau of Transportation Statistics,
March 2003. www.bts.gov/publications/issue_briefs/
number_01/pdf/entire.pdf.

11. "Household Vehicles Energy Use: Latest Data &
Trends" [online]. [Cited January 27, 2006]. United
States Energy Information Administration, November
2005. www.cia.doc.gov/emeu/rtecs/nhts_survey/2001/
index.html.

12. "Energy and Environment" [online]. [Cited January 27,
2006]. American Public Transit Association. http://apta.
com/research/stats/factbook/documents/energy.pdf.

13. "National Fuel Price Crisis Watch: Fuel Talking Points" [online]. [Cited February 7, 2006]. American Trucking Associations. www.truckline.com/fuelpricecrisis/talking points.

14. Renee Montagne. "Interview: David Field on Katrina's impact on airline industry" [online]. [Cited January 27, 2006]. Morning Edition, National Public Radio, September 2, 2005. http://search.epnet.com/login.aspx? direct=true&db=nfh&an=6XN200509021110.

15. Lester Brown. *Outgrowing the Earth: The Food Security Challenge in an Age of Falling Water Tables and Rising Temperatures.* Norton & Norton, 2004, p. 4.

16. Patricia S. Muir. "Trends in Pesticide Use" [online]. Oregon State University, BI301 Human Impacts on Ecosystems, Fall 2005. http://oregonstate.edu/~muirp/pesttren.htm.

17. David Pimentel and Mario Giampietro. "Food, Land, Population and the U.S. Economy: Executive Summary" [online]. [Cited February 17, 2006]. Carrying Capacity Network, November 21, 1994. www.dieoff.com/page40.htm.

18. Dale Allen Pfeiffer. "Eating Fossil Fuels" [online]. [Cited February 17, 2006]. From The Wilderness Publications, 2004. www.fromthewilderness.com/free/ww3/100303_eating_oil.html.

19. Danielle Murray. "Rising oil prices will impact food supplies" [online]. September 13, 2005. www.people andplanet.net/doc.php?id=2532.

20. "Grazing Lands: RCA Issue Brief #6" [online]. United States Department of Agriculture, National Resources Conservations Service, November 1995. www.nrcs.usda .gov/technical/land/pubs/ib6text.html#multiple.

21. Jimmy Westerfeld. "Agriculture facing its own Katrina" [online]. [Cited February 17, 2006]. Texas Farm Bureau, October 21, 2005. www.txfb.org/TexasAgriculture/2005/102105/102105opinions.htm.

22. Glenn Frankel. "U.S. Mulled Seizing Oil Fields in '73" [online]. [Cited April 9, 2006]. *Washington Post,* January 1, 2004. www.washingtonpost.com/ac2/wp-dyn?page name = article&node = &contentId = A46321-2003Dec 31&notFound = true.

23. "Vice President Cheney's Speech to the Veterans of Foreign Wars" [online]. [Cited February 17, 2006]. Project for the New American Century, August 26, 2002. www.newamericancentury.org/iraq-082602.htm.

24. Andrea R. Mihailescu. "Analysis: Oil still a lucrative business" [online]. [Cited February 17, 2006]. United Press International, January 1, 2006. www.upi.com/InternationalIntelligence/view.php?StoryID = 2005 1230-114541-4540r.

25. Major Chris L. Jeffries. "NATO and Oil: Conflict and Capabilities" [online]. [Cited February 17, 2006]. Air University Review, January-February 1980, posted January 30, 2002. www.airpower.au.af.mil/airchronicles/aureview/1980/jan-feb/jefferies.html.

26. Strategic Defence Review [online]. [Cited November 1, 2005]. www.mod.uk/issues/sdr/newchapter/Causes_Counter_Strategies.htm. This link has expired, however the review is discussed at http://theyworkforyou.com/debates/?id = 2002-07-18.460.0&s = terrorism + speaker %3A10312.

27. Mohammed Alkhereiji. "Bin Laden moves toward economic terror" [online]. [Cited March 4, 2006]. The Daily Star (Beirut), January 24, 2005. www.dailystar

.com.lb/article.asp?edition_id=10&categ_id=5&
article_id=12002.

28. Ibid.

29. Christopher M. Blanchard. "Al Qaeda: Statements and
Evolving Ideology" [online]. [Cited February 17, 2006].
Congressional Research Service, Report for Congress,
June 20, 2005. http://images.usnews.com/usnews/news/
articles/050622/alqaeda_crs.pdf.

Chapter 3: A Plan

1. Hugh Rockoff. "Price Controls" [online]. [Cited February 17, 2006]. *The Concise Encyclopedia of Economics.*
Library of Economics and Liberty, 2002.
www.econlib.org/library/Enc/PriceControls.html.

2. Jim Cox. "Price Controls" [online]. [Cited February 17,
2006]. The Concise Guide to Economics. Savannah-
Pikeville Press, 1997. http://freedomkeys.com/price
controls3.htm.

3. Jan Rocha. "Brazil announces energy rationing" [on-
line]. [Cited February 17, 2006]. BBC News Online,
May 29, 2001. http://news.bbc.co.uk/1/hi/world/
americas/1339133.stm.

4. "Kyoto Protocol—Details of the Agreement" [online].
[Cited April 15, 2006]. http://en.wikipedia.org/wiki/
Kyoto_Protocol.

5. "Contraction and Convergence: A Global Solution to a
Global Problem" [online]. [Cited February 17, 2006].
Global Commons Institute. www.gci.org.uk/contconv/
cc.html#intro.

6. C&C envisions:
   • A full-term contraction budget for global emissions

consistent with stabilizing atmospheric concentrations of greenhouse gases (GHGs) at a pre-agreed concentration maximum deemed to be safe, following IPCC WGi carbon cycle modeling. (GCI sees higher than 450 parts per million by volume [ppmv] CO_2 equivalent as "not-safe").

• The international sharing of this budget as "entitlements" results from a negotiable rate of linear convergence to equal shares per person globally by an agreed date within the timeline of the full-term contraction/concentration agreement. GCI suggests (a) between the years 2020 and 2050, or around a third of the way into a 100 year budget, for example, for convergence to complete and (b) that a population base-year in the C&C schedule is agreed.

• The inter-regional, inter-national and intranational tradability of these entitlements in an appropriate currency such as International Energy Backed Currency Units (EBCUs - 5) should be encouraged.

• Scientific understanding of the relationship between an emissions-free economy and concentrations develops, so rates of C&C can evolve under periodic revision.

• "GCI Briefing: Contraction and Convergence" [online]. [Cited February 17, 2006]. Global Commons Institute. www.gci.org.uk/briefings/ICE.pdf.

6. "Climate and Currency: Proposals for Global Monetary Reform" [online]. [Cited February 17, 2006]. FEASTA. www.Feasta.org/documents/moneyecology/money proposals.htm#top.

7. Published previously under the titles The Rimini Protocol or The Uppsala Protocol.

8. American sustainability activist Jack Santa-Barbara has authored an alternative Oil Depletion Protocol, currently unpublished.

9. Jean Laherrère. "Review on Oil Shale Data" [online]. [Cited February 17, 2006]. September 2005. www.hub bertpeak.com/laherrere/OilShaleReview200509.pdf; see also Spencer Reiss. "Tapping the Rock Field" [online]. [Cited February 17, 2006]. *WIRED Magazine,* December 2005. www.wired.com/wired/archive/13.12/oilshale.html.

Chapter 4: Dealing with Diminishing Oil

1. "Price of Gas" [online]. [Cited March 13, 2006]. Scien-Central News, July, 28, 2005. www.sciencentral.com/articles/view.php3?article_id=218392605&cat=all.

2. Paul Mobbs. *Energy Beyond Oil: Could You Cut Your Energy Use by Sixty Per Cent?* Matador, 2005, p. 116. For more discussion of the relative benefits and impacts of biodiesel production, see: N. D. Mortimer, P. Cormack, M. A. Elsayed and R. E. Horne. "Evaluation of the Comparative Energy, Global Warming, and Socio-Economic Costs and Benefits of Biodiesel" [online]. [Cited February 26, 2006]. Resources research unit, School of Environment and Development, Sheffield Hallam University, January 2003. www.shu.ac.uk/rru/projects/biodiesel_evaluation.html; George Monbiot. "The most destructive crop on earth is no solution to the energy crisis" [online]. [Cited February 26, 2006]. *Guardian Unlimited,* December 6, 2005. www.guardian.co.uk/print/0,3858,5349045-103390,00.html.

3. David Pimentel and Tad W. Patzek. "Ethanol Production

Using Corn, Switchgrass, and Wood; Biodiesel Production Using Soybean and Sunflower" [online]. *Natural Resources Research,* 14, no. 1 (March 2005). http://petro leum.berkeley.edu/papers/Biofuels/NRRethanol.2005 .pdf.

4. Hosein Shapouri, James A. Duffield, and Michael S. Graboski. "Estimating the Net Energy Balance of Corn Ethanol" [online]. [Cited February 26, 2006]. *Agricultural Economic Report No. 721.,* U.S. Department of Agriculture, Economic Research Service, Office of Energy, July 1995. www.ers.usda.gov/publications/aer721/AER 721.PDF.

5. Alexander E. Farrell, Richard J. Plevin, Brian T. Turner, Andrew D. Jones, Michael O'Hare, Daniel M. Kammen. "Ethanol Can Contribute to Energy and Environmental Goals" [online]. [Cited February 26, 2006]. *Science,* 311 no. 5760 January 27, 2006. http://rael.berkeley.edu/ EBAMM/.

6. Steve Koonin. "Getting Serious About Biofuels." *Science,* 311 no. 5760 (January 27, 2006): 435. See also: Arthur J. Ragauskas, et al. "The Path Forward for Biofuels and Biomaterials." *Science* 311 no. 5760 (January 27, 2006): 484–489. Abstract: "Biomass represents an abundant carbon-neutral renewable resource for the production of bioenergy and biomaterials, and its enhanced use would address several societal needs. Advances in genetics, biotechnology, process chemistry, and engineering are leading to a new manufacturing concept for converting renewable biomass to valuable fuels and products, generally referred to as the biorefinery. The integration of agroenergy crops and biorefinery manufacturing tech-

nologies offers the potential for the development of sustainable biopower and biomaterials that will lead to a new manufacturing paradigm."

7. A reply article by Tad Patzek of the University of California, Berkeley, privately distributed, was unpublished at the time of this writing.

8. Kamol Sukin. "Alternative Fuel: Gasohol pumps may soon be running dry" [online]. [Cited February 26, 2006]. *The Nation*, January 29, 2006. http://nationmulti-media.com/2006/01/29/headlines/index.php?news=headlines_19778465.html. See also: Devlin Buckley. "Ethanol: a dangerous trend" [online]. [Cited February 26, 2006]. *Online Journal*, January 25, 2006. http://onlinejournal.com/artman/publish/article_451.shtml.

9. Mycle Schneider. "A Dose of Reality for Those Greens Going Nuclear: Combating global warming with nuclear energy is wishful thinking" [online]. [Cited February 26, 2006]. Utne.com, April 21, 2005. www.utne.com/webwatch/2005_195/news/11620-1.html.

10. However, there is a recently identified problem of ozone destruction in the high atmosphere from the accidental release of free hydrogen at ground level. See www.theozonehole.com/hydrogeneconomy.htm.

11. Baldur Eliasson and Ulf Bossel. "The Future of the Hydrogen Economy: Bright or Bleak?" [online]. [Cited March 4, 2006]. www.woodgas.com/hydrogen_economy.pdf.

12. "The Hydrogen Economy: Opportunities, Costs, Barriers, and R&D Needs" [online]. [Cited February 26, 2006]. Committee on Alternatives and Strategies for Future Hydrogen Production and Use, National

Research Council, National Academy of Engineering, 2004. http://books.nap.edu/catalog/10922.html?onpi_newsdoc02042004.

13. "Saving Oil in a Hurry: Measures for Rapid Demand Restraint in Transport" [online]. [Cited February 26, 2006]. International Energy Agency, February 28, 2005. www.stcwa.org.au/journal/210405/files/background_IEA.pdf.

14. "Saving Oil in a Hurry," p. x.

15. "Saving Oil in a Hurry," p. 17.

16. "Saving Oil in a Hurry," p. 22.

17. See the Casual Carpool FAQ at www.ridenow.org/carpool/what.htm.

18. "Ride-Share: A Modest Proposal" [online]. [Cited February 26, 2006]. The Community Solution. www.communitysolution.org/rideshare.html.

19. See www.ridenow.org.

20. See Guaranteed Ride Home at http://rideshare.511.org/rideshare_rewards/guaranteed.asp.

21. Eric Pryne. "Can 'hitchhiking' help commuters? Consultant seeks to ease congestion" [online]. [Cited February 26, 2006]. *Seattle Times,* November 18, 2004. http://seattletimes.nwsource.com/html/localnews/2002094189_hitchhike18m.html.

22. See Go Geronimo at www.gogeronimo.org/Home/Home.html.

23. See, for example, various proposals for some form of "personal rapid transit" at http://faculty.washington.edu/jbs/itrans/prtquick.htm.

24. Jane Holtz Kay. *Asphalt Nation.* Crown, 1997, pp. 304–305.

25. Holtz Kay, p. 296.
26. "Smartcode: a comprehensive form-based planning ordinance" [online]. [Cited February 26, 2006]. Duany Plater-Zyberk & Company, and Municipal Code Corporation, Spring 2005. http://tndtownpaper.com/images/ SmartCode6.5.pdf.
27. Holtz Kay, p. 343.
28. Personal communication, January 2006.
29. From Table 2 of www.usda.gov/oce/oepnu/net%20 energy%20balance.doc [Cited March 4, 2006]; another version of the same study, with somewhat different numbers, is cited elsewhere as being at www.ethanol-gec.org/ corn_eth.htm [link expired] or www.usda.gov/oce/ reports/energy/aer-814.pdf [Cited March 4, 2006].
30. David Holmgren. *Permaculture: Principles and Pathways Beyond Sustainability.* Holmgren Design Services, 2002, p. 38. For more information on the agricultural applications of brown coal see Stephen W. Kline and Charles E. Wilson. "Proposal for Experimentation with Arkansas Lignite to Identify Organic Soil Supplements Suitable to Regional Agricultural Needs" [online]. [Cited February 26, 2006]. Arkansas Tech University, January 26, 1994. www.atu.edu/acad/mining/people/misk/lignite.htm.
31. Calvin Frouche, Mark Gaskell, Steven T. Koike, Jeff Mitchell, and Richard Smith. "Insect Pest Management for Organic Crops" [online]. [Cited February 26, 2006]. Vegetable Research and Information Center, University of California, Davis. http://anrcatalog.ucdavis.edu/pdf/ 7251.pdf.
32. John B. Campbell. "New Markets for Bio-Based Energy and Industrial Feedstocks: Biodiesel—Will There Be Enough?" [online]. [Cited February 26, 2006]. Agricul-

tural Outlook Forum 2000, Feb 25, 2000. www.usda
.gov/oce/waob/Archives/2000/speeches/campbell.txt.
According to a study written by Drs. Van Dyne and
Raymer for the Tennessee Valley Authority ("Biodiesel
Production Potential from Industrial Rapeseed in the
Southeastern U.S." [online]. Southeastern Regional
Biomass Energy Program administered by the Tennessee
Valley Authority, TV-86444V, October 31, 1992. www
.biodiesel.org/resources/reportsdatabase/reports/gen/
19921031_gen-239.pdf), the average US farm consumes
fuel at the rate of 82 liters per hectare (8.75 US gallons per
acre) of land to produce one crop. However, average
crops of rapeseed produce oil at an average rate of 1,029
L/ha (110 US gal/acre), and high-yield rapeseed fields
produce about 1,356 L/ha (145 US gal/acre). The ratio of
input to output in these cases is roughly 1:12.5 and 1:16.5.
Photosynthesis is known to have an efficiency rate of
about 16 percent and if the entire mass of a crop is utilized for energy production, the overall efficiency of this
chain is known to be about one percent. This does not
compare favorably to solar cells combined with an electric drive train. Biodiesel out-competes solar cells in cost
and ease of deployment. However, these statistics by
themselves are not enough to show whether such a
change makes economic sense.

33. "Organic Corn & Soy Yields Comparable to Conventional" [online]. Organic Consumers Association, April
4, 2003. www.organicconsumers.org/organic/041903_
organic.cfm.

"Agronomy Journal Scientists from the University of
Minnesota demonstrated yields of corn and soybeans
were only minimally reduced when organic production

practices were utilized as compared with conventional production practices. After factoring in production costs, net returns between the two production strategies were equivalent. For a total of 154 growing seasons for different crops, grown in different parts of [the United States] on both rain-fed and irrigated land, organic production yielded 95% of crops grown under conventional high-input conditions." Bill Liebhardt. "Get the facts straight: Organic agriculture yields are good" [online]. [Cited February 26, 2006]. Organic Farming Research Foundation 10 (Summer 2001). www.ofrf.org/ publications/news/IB10.pdf.

34. Helena Norberg-Hodge, Todd Merrifield and Steven Gorelick. *Bringing the Food Economy Home: Local Alternatives to Global Agribusiness*. Kumarian Press, 2002.

35. According to Norberg-Hodge et al., direct farm subsidies in the United States, for example, rise with the amount of land a farmer has. Consequently in the year 2000, the largest 10% of US farms received almost two-thirds of federal subsidies available—around $17 billion. Recipients of those subsidies include a number of Fortune 500 companies such as Archer Daniels Midland and Chevron. In Europe, the situation is similar: 80% of UK farm subsidies are given to 20% of farmers, again those with the largest holdings.

Chapter 5. Discussion of the Protocol

1. Hirsch, *op. cit.,* p. 6.

2. USGS World Energy Assessment Team. "U.S. Geological Survey World Petroleum Assessment 2000—Description and Results" [online]. [Cited February 27, 2006]. US Department of the Interior, US Geological Survey. http://pubs.usgs.gov/dds/dds-060/.

3. Thanks to petroleum geologist Jeffrey J. Brown for pointing out this dilemma. See www.energybulletin.net/13575.html [Cited April 11, 2006].

4. David Fleming. *Energy and the Common Purpose.* The Lean Economy Connection, 2005. See also www.teqs .net/.

5. Hirsch, *op. cit.,* p. 66.

Chapter 6: How Can the Protocol Be Adopted?

1. Mona Sahlin. "Sweden first to break dependence on oil!" [online]. [Cited February 27, 2006]. Government Offices of Sweden,October 1, 2005. www.sweden.gov .se/sb/d/3212/a/51058. See also Lars Olofsson. "Swedish government embraces peak oil and looks towards bio-fuels" [online]. [Cited February 27, 2006]. EnergyBul-letin, December 17, 2005. www.energybulletin.net/11759 .html.

2. "Launch of Forfás Oil Dependency Study" [online]. [Cited April 9, 2006]. www.forfas.ie/news.asp?page_id =366.

3. "Peak Oil resolution in the U.S. House of Representa-tives" [online]. [Cited February 27, 2006]. ASPO USA, November 23, 2005. www.aspo-usa.com/news.cfm?nd =1423.

4. "President Bush Delivers State of the Union Address" [online]. [Cited February 27, 2006]. United States, January 31, 2006. www.whitehouse.gov/news/releases/ 2006/01/20060131-10.html.

5. "Face the Nation" [online]. CBS-TV News interview with Bob Schieffer, January 29, 2006. www.cbsnews .com/stories/2005/07/25/podcast_nation/main711465 .shtml.

6. Alister Doyle. "Iceland's hydrogen buses zip toward oil-

free economy" [online]. [Cited February 27, 2006]. *Detroit News*, Reuters. www.detnews.com/2005/autos insider/0501/14/autos-60181.htm.

7. Gareth Doutch. "Peak Oil And The Politics Of Global Solutions" [online]. Peak Oil and Simpol blog, January 7, 2006. www.countercurrents.org/pa-doutch070106 .htm. See also The Simultaneous Policy at www.simpol .org.

8. Howard T. Odum and Elizabeth C. Odum. *The Prosperous Way Down: Principles and Policies.* University Press of Colorado, 2001. This term is used throughout. e.g., Part III of the book is titled "Policies for Transition and Descent."

9. "Kinsale 2021 An Energy Descent Action Plan" [online]. [Cited February 27, 2006]. Edited by Rob Hopkins. Kinsale Further Education College, 2005. http:// transition culture.org/?p = 129.

10. John Hickenlooper talks about peak oil during ASPO USA conference (transcript), January 8 2006. www.globalpublicmedia.com/transcripts/618.

11. "Recommendations towards Energy Independence for the City of Willits and Surrounding Community" [online]. [Cited February 27, 2006]. Willits Economic Localization (WELL) and Willits Ad-Hoc Energy Group, August 29, 2005. www.willitseconomiclocalization.org/ Papers/EnergyIndependencePlan.pdf.

12. "Global Peak in Oil Production: The Municipal Context" [online]. [Cited February 27, 2006]. Council Report from the Transportation Committee, Meeting, January 16, 2006. http://burnaby.fileprosite.com/ contentengine/document.asp?Print = yes&ID = 9181.

13. See City Repair at www.cityrepair.org/about.html.

INDEX

Page numbers followed by fig indicate figures.

ABOUT THE AUTHOR

RICHARD HEINBERG is one of the world's foremost Peak Oil educators. He is the award-winning author of seven books including *The Party's Over: Oil, War and the Fate of Industrial Societies; Powerdown: Options and Actions for a Post-Carbon World.* He is a Core Faculty member of New College of California, where he teaches a program on "Culture, Ecology and Sustainable Community." His monthly *MuseLetter* has been published since 1992 and his essays and articles have appeared widely, and in many languages. He was featured prominently in the documentary film *The End of Suburbia,* he has been quoted in *Time* magazine, and his work has been discussed in articles syndicated by Reuters and the Associated Press. Since 2002, he has given over two hundred lectures on oil depletion ("Peak Oil") to a wide variety of audiences—from insurance executives to peace activists, from local and national elected officials to Jesuit volunteers. He and his wife Janet Barocco live in Santa Rosa, CA, in an energy-efficient home. He is also an avid amateur violinist.

If you have enjoyed *The Oil Depletion Protocol* you might also enjoy other

BOOKS TO BUILD A NEW SOCIETY

Our books provide positive solutions for people who want to
make a difference. We specialize in:

Environment and Justice • Conscientious Commerce
Sustainable Living • Ecological Design and Planning
Natural Building & Appropriate Technology • New Forestry
Educational and Parenting Resources • Nonviolence
Progressive Leadership • Resistance and Community

New Society Publishers

ENVIRONMENTAL BENEFITS STATEMENT

New Society Publishers has chosen to produce this book on Enviro 100, recycled
paper made with **100% post consumer waste**, processed chlorine free, and old
growth free.

For every 5,000 books printed, New Society saves the following resources:[1]

25	Trees
2,283	Pounds of Solid Waste
2,512	Gallons of Water
3,276	Kilowatt Hours of Electricity
4,150	Pounds of Greenhouse Gases
18	Pounds of HAPs, VOCs, and AOX Combined
6	Cubic Yards of Landfill Space

[1]Environmental benefits are calculated based on research done by the Environmental Defense Fund and
other members of the Paper Task Force who study the environmental impacts of the paper industry.

For a full list of NSP's titles, please call 1-800-567-6772 *or check out our website at:*

www.newsociety.com

NEW SOCIETY PUBLISHERS